Seek the
Happy
Life

**PAUL H.
DUNN**

Seek the Happy Life

PAUL H. DUNN

Bookcraft
Salt Lake City, Utah

Library of Congress Catalog Card Number: 85-70242
ISBN 0-88494-553-7

8th Printing, 1990

Printed in the United States of America

Preface

Ask any person what he wants most and his response will usually involve things he considers essential to happiness. Ask him what constitutes happiness and you will probably receive a variety of answers. Our society is so ordered that we all work very hard at achieving things, at getting things done, or at getting material things. But things are often the antithesis of happiness; and that's the choice we so often face—real joy or things, true happiness or possessions.

To each has been given the miraculous gift of life. For the gloomy thinker life seems to be a painful, daily routine. For others, it is a God-given opportunity intended to be a self-fulfilling experience in discovering values and principles which lead to eternal life. Happy people accept success, disappointments, mystery, tragedy, sorrow, joy, and still love life. Happy people try to live every moment fully.

A person whom I have not been able to identify has written the following: "Happiness is a journey, not a destination. Happiness is to be found along the way, not at the end of the road . . . for then the journey is over and it is too late. The time for happiness is today, not tomorrow."

The gospel contains the "happy news," and this book is another attempt by the author to teach and share gospel truths in such a way that the reader can make a more practical application to life and thus find greater joy and happiness.

This volume is not endorsed by The Church of Jesus Christ of Latter-day Saints and I alone am responsible for its contents. I hereby absolve the Church and its leaders from any responsibility for errors contained herein.

As always I am most grateful to many for this publication. I express particular thanks to my wife, Jeanne, and daughters, Janet and Marsha, for their insights and editorial assistance. I am so very appreciative to my secretary, Colleen Erickson, for many hours of proofreading and for typing the manuscript. Special thanks to my friend, David Christensen, for his many suggestions and help.

As in times past, I express deep gratitude to my companion, Jeanne, and daughters, Janet, Marsha, and Kellie and their families for constant support and encouragement.

Paul H. Dunn

Contents

Part Three: In Opposition

Part Four: In Living

Seek and Ye Shall Find

I have the opportunity as an officer of the Church to travel much of the world. It is exciting, it is interesting, and it is challenging. Quite frequently, as we go to and fro—and once in a while even in the ranks of our own people—we will hear the comment, "Boy, the world is sure going to the dogs." Think about that for a minute. I couldn't help but pull from my notebook this little statement by an author I have not been able to identify:

My granddad, viewing earth's worn cogs,
Said, "Things are going to the dogs."
His granddad, in his house of logs,
Said, "Things are going to the dogs."
His granddad, in the Flemish bogs,
Said, "Things are going to the dogs."
His granddad, in the old skin togs,
Said, "Things are going to the dogs."

There is one thing I have to state:
"The dogs have had a good long wait."

As one of the witnesses of our Lord, I feel that that time has not yet arrived. I think we have a great future. I want to assure you that with all the ups and downs in the world today, what you and I are doing here in preparation for life is essential. I am one of your supporters and cheer you on as you make necessary and marvelous preparations.

I have often thought, as I have watched young people throughout the Church, What a wonderful time it is to be alive and to know what an impact you are having on the world! Don't you agree? If you had to choose the time in which you would be a young or a more mature adult, which era would you pick? Think about it. Would you go back to some of the generations that your parents represent? grandparents? I was a teenager and a young adult in the forties. Would that be a decade you would choose? If you think the world looks bleak today, you should have seen it in the forties.

Let's talk about that a little. Not so much about the forties, but about what you are, where you are, and the future that lies before you. If you and I had an opportunity for a few moments to sit one-to-one—and I would like that—there are four things I might like to share with you as you contemplate your present circumstances and think about the future.

First, I might want to discuss with you the fact that you are literally an offspring of heavenly parents—you really are—and you came into mortality to succeed. You are not a failure. Failure is simply an outgrowth of lack of confidence or understanding. As your friend, I testify that you have brilliance and divinity within you. It is being tested; it always has been and always will be. As you plan for the future, consider very seriously what the Lord has already instilled in you. A lot of young people say, "I'm not sure what I want to do in life." Now, of course, is the time to ponder that and experiment a little bit. The Lord has already told you, in part, what you should do.

Let me ask you a few questions. What are your desires? What are you good at? What usually comes quite easily for you? What do you enjoy doing most? What spiritual gifts do you have? Tonight, sometime before you retire, would you do yourself a favor? Read and reread section 46 of the Doctrine and Covenants. It won't take long, and from it you will gain tremendous insight concerning your divine potential, for the Lord has indeed blessed you spiritually with gifts that are unique, that are different from those of any other person in the world. You came with blessings earned and talents developed before you entered mortality.

If we could be in a classroom arrangement and I asked you to name ten things that you would like to accomplish by your fortieth birthday (I know forty seems like time and all eternity away, but it really isn't), I would be intensely interested in what you would mention. In that list you would be telling me the things you like to do and would be good at. Quite frequently a parent will want to train a child to take over his or her profession. That may be well and good, and maybe you would like to follow along in your parent's occupation, but ponder carefully what unique talents and abilities you have. They may be quite different from those of others in your family.

All my boyhood days I wanted to be an athlete. That was all I could think about. I ate, drank, and slept sports. I had a wonderful father, who was in the grocery business. By the time I was a teenager he had developed a chain of grocery stores, and in those stores he was training his boys to have a skill to offer to the world. My older brother didn't want it. He wanted to be a teacher. My younger brother wanted to be a doctor. I wanted to be an athlete. Our father was wise enough not to pressure or force any of us into a given profession. He said, "I have developed these stores so that you could learn and would always have a skill. If you don't want it, I will sell all the stores." And he did, that quickly! Each of us went on to pursue another profession, but we all have training in something we could fall back on if we needed to.

As a good parent, he considered first the unique needs of his sons rather than merely trying to fulfill his own desires. Ponder these things; seek the counsel of your parents, wise bishops, leaders, and friends in whom you have trust.

The second point is, if you don't already have it, secure your patriarchal blessing. Do it with spiritual orientation and understanding and preparation. I always like to think of a patriarchal blessing as personal scripture, because the Lord is there revealing to each of us those things that are potentially good and great in our lives, and they can all be fulfilled if we meet certain qualifications and conditions.

At the risk of personal embarrassment I share this experience. When I was a young teenager wanting to pursue the athletic life, I was moving along with relative ease and with some accomplishment. The time came when I signed a professional baseball contract. Unfortunately, world conditions were very serious. Most of the world was engaged in a conflict, and then suddenly the Japanese attacked the United States. It became necessary that year to draft millions of young men into military service and to eventually lower the draft age to eighteen. I turned eighteen the very month it was changed. How was that for timing? Each young man was given a draft number, and the government had a national drawing in Washington to see which numbers would go first. Do I have to tell you whose number they picked? Instead of going into sports I ended up in the military.

My dad, upon learning that I was to be in that first eighteen-year-old draft, called me to his side and said, "Paul, you haven't yet received your patriarchal blessing. Would you like to do that?" He gave me some good spiritual preparation, and being a typical youth I said, "Yeah, I'll do it." I went and got the necessary recommend, and on the appointed day I made preparation to have the blessing. My dad made one other suggestion. I Ie said, "Maybe you would like to fast and pray about it before you go." Well, for me to fast one meal in those days was monumental, but somehow I got through it, had a private prayer about certain concerns I had regarding my future, and then drove to the stake center.

Brother George Wride, Los Angeles Stake patriarch, was there to receive me. He was in his eighties, white haired, and not sure of foot. Now, you know what an eighty-year-old man looks like to a teenager. I thought I was being blessed by Abraham. He came out of the office to get my recommend, and as I looked at him I thought, "Boy, this will be some experience!"

He took my recommend, ushered me into the office, had me sit down, and then pulled up a chair so that we were quite close to each other. I thought he had one foot in that office and the other foot in heaven. Then he gave me a very thorough interview, and after about twenty minutes he stood up, came around behind me, and put his hands on my head. He called me by name, declared my lineage, and then paused. I'll never forget what followed. He said, "Now concerning the future, thou shalt experience combat in the military. Angels shall intercede in thy behalf and protect thee all the days of thy life, and thou shalt live many years and will testify to all nations of the world that Jesus is the Christ." He then continued to tell me some very personal things. All of it was in concert with the desires of my heart as I had expressed them earlier when I knelt to pray to God.

Well, I went home after that, and even *I* was impressed. You know how parents are—very anxious about what happens to their kids—so when I walked in the door my dad said, "What did he say? What did he say?"

I said, "I don't know; he had angels flying around." I guess, though impressed, I still lacked a little understanding.

Two weeks later my blessing came in the mail. Now, my father, as a young married man, had taught at Brigham Young University when it was on the lower campus. He taught typing, shorthand, and penmanship, and he was so good at these skills that the year he died, at age sixty-four, he could still type 120 words a minute on a conventional typewriter. When the blessing came, then, quite naturally he sat down at the typewriter and, unbeknown to me—tap, tap, tap—produced a copy of it. He purchased a waterproof wallet, put the blessing inside, and handed it to me, saying, "Now, take it with you and read it often."

I'm hesitant to tell you that I went off to war and during ten months of training in the United States I didn't even open the wallet. After our training in the States had ended, I was shipped to Hawaii for three additional months of jungle training. Then at four o'clock one morning we were loaded onto troopships, and away we went to an undisclosed destination.

Three weeks later we found ourselves in a harbor where the navy was pounding a beach with heavy artillery fire. You've seen enough war movies to understand a little of how it is done. The night before the invasion we were issued live ammunition. Now, all of a sudden, the previous year's training came into focus. Most of us were young—I had just had my nineteenth birthday—and not as confident as we tried to appear. We didn't go below deck that night because we were all frightened, wondering what was expected of us. The next morning I was assigned to the seventh boat team—the seventh wave, as it was called. We started to load into the landing craft at about 0500 (5:00 A.M.); 0600 (6:00 A.M.) was to be H-hour on D-day.

I don't know if you understand the challenge of getting into a landing craft. It is interesting. The deck where we were standing was about four stories above the water, and the sea that morning was quite rough—we were experiencing forty-foot swells—and we were attempting to get into these landing craft (LCVPs) which held thirty infantrymen each. In heavy seas the craft would sway back and forth, hitting the side of the ship, and then drop as much as forty feet in the swells. One by one we had to climb down the ship's side on a cargo net and then time our drop into the small boat as it banged against the side of the ship. Keep in mind that each of us was carrying a twenty-pound pack, a ten-pound rifle, a five-pound helmet, thirty-five pounds of ammunition, and as if that weren't enough, all the characters above us on the cargo nets were stepping on our fingers. Because that equipment weighed so much, if any man dropped at the wrong moment and missed the boat he likely wouldn't surface again.

From the time we arrived in the harbor until just a few seconds before H-hour, the navy pounded the beach with explosives in order to prepare for the infantry invasion. The noise from the shells was so loud that we couldn't even hear each other talk while sitting next to one another. It was deafening. Pretty soon we started to click off our watches—five minutes before H-hour, four, three, two, one. Exactly as the second hand passed the mark, the navy ceased firing. There was total silence on the water. Thousands of men were present, but no one was making a sound.

At that very moment a flare went off, signaling the launch of the first boat team. The boats were approximately two thousand yards from shore. When they were twelve hundred yards away, the quiet of the moment was shattered by a thunder of enemy fire coming from the beach. One craft after another was hit, scattering American soldiers into the water.

A second flare went off signaling the launch of the next wave. The enemy fire continued through the second, third, fourth, fifth, and sixth waves. No one had managed to get ashore.

The hour we spent waiting for our turn was a sobering experience.

Finally a flare went up signaling the launch of the seventh wave—my boat team. It was eerie sitting there in that boat, going up and down in the water as we neared the beach. I could see the palm trees getting larger. My heart was pounding as loudly as the enemy firing that continued as we approached.

It was now H-hour plus one, and the tide was beginning to go out. In the process, a large piece of coral reef was exposed and our landing craft struck it and became lodged. The navy crew grew excited and dropped the front of the boat saying, "Get out of here! Get out! You're drawing fire!"

We jumped into the water, which was about chest high. We had to hold our rifles over our heads to keep the muzzles dry—salt water could cause a rifle to blow up when fired. Have you ever tried to run in five feet of water while you were loaded down with heavy equipment? You don't move very fast.

While the enemy continued to fire on us, we were forced to use the butts of our rifles to push aside some of the bodies of the dead. At the same time, we did what we could to help our wounded friends and associates, men with whom we had trained for a year. To make matters worse, the coral rock on the reef was so sharp it cut through our boots, causing our feet to bleed. The shore seemed hopelessly out of reach.

Somehow I was one of the first ashore that morning, and I dug my first foxhole with my hands and fingernails. As I crawled into that hole, an enemy ambu gun opened up on my position. An ambu gun could shoot about seven hundred rounds a minute. One bullet went down my right arm and took off my identification bracelet. I want you to know that at that point I began to think about life, its purposes, and my Heavenly Father. I wanted to know why I had to be in this situation. I needed some answers.

Later, as we secured the beach, I reached into my pocket, took out that wallet containing my patriarchal blessing, and read what the Lord had said: "Angels shall intercede in thy behalf and protect thee all the days of thy life, and thou shalt live many years and will testify to all nations of the world that Jesus is the Christ." Imagine what that meant to me out there. I rolled over and sought my Heavenly Father, and in that critical moment he answered me. I have not been the same since.

Get a patriarchal blessing, young people. Ponder it. At this stage of my life, it is exciting for me to read in mine what the Lord said when I was a teenager, and to see the fulfillment of those promises and blessings.

Take the time to ponder your desires, your interests, and talents, and couple them with your blessing. They go hand in hand—they really do.

The third idea I would want to relate to you is the wisdom of seeking the counsel and advice of those you respect and honor. Both in and out of the Church there are many people who, because of their experience and training, can give you much help in your preparation. Think of the untapped resources available to you today. It is sad to note how few young people take the opportunity to learn from those who are experts in their fields.

I'm not for a minute trying to suggest what you ought to do as a career. I don't know. Perhaps you want to be a doctor, a lawyer, an architect, a designer. Who knows?

You do, and the Lord does. It would seem very logical to seek the counsel of those who could give you the kind of understanding and preparation you need to succeed. Truly great people always take time to assist. People of lesser character never seem to have the time.

When I attended the university some years ago, I noticed an interesting pattern among young people who were trying to decide their individual futures. By the junior year, the average student will have shifted his major three times. Does that tell you anything? Why not take the time earlier to determine the direction you want to go? Many times I have sat in counsel with a student who went into engineering when he really wanted to be a doctor. One man thought he wanted to be a ballplayer until the pro sport became a part of his life and it wasn't what he thought it ought to be. Perhaps what you have in mind is exactly what you should do, but maybe the matter needs more thought and planning.

Sometimes I have the opportunity to play in golf tournaments that are supported by celebrities. In one tournament in North Carolina I was playing a round with Willie Mays, the former great hitter from the New York and San Francisco Giants. As we played the course we talked about many things. Baseball was a dominant subject. We covered many aspects of the game. At the appropriate moment I asked him a personal question, "Willie," I said, "in the years since your retirement how many Little Leaguers and college and high school athletes who have a desire to one day play major league ball have sought your personal counsel on the art of hitting?"

He answered, "Nobody. I get lots of requests for autographs, but no requests for counsel and advice."

I said, "What?"

Keep in mind, I was talking with one of the greatest baseball players of all time. Fifteen million boys in America are preparing for a major league baseball career (remember there are only eight hundred openings), and yet none of them have sought the counsel of one of the greatest authorities in the world.

Can you imagine living in the day of Shakespeare and wanting to be a writer, and not taking time to get his counsel? Can you imagine wanting to be an artist and living down the street from Michelangelo, and not inquiring concerning the secret of his genius?

People you regard as exemplary are often so busy that you may feel uncomfortable in asking for an interview. But young people who courteously make and keep appointments, and who are humble (teachable) in their search for information and guidance, are a pleasure to counsel. Think of the many retired people whose expertise is never tapped.

The fourth point, and probably the most important one, is to cultivate a personal relationship with your Heavenly Father. Seek him for counsel and direction in governing your life.

Our Heavenly Father has sent us here to learn how to become like him. But he isn't going to do all our homework for us. That is our job. A lot of young people come to me and say, "Well, Elder Dunn, I pray and I don't get any answers." My question is, "How do you pray?" Maybe you are the way my little girls were some years ago. They would want me to do their homework while they watched TV. I hope a wise father would never do that, but instead would say something like: "You go and study it out. You go and do the problems and bring them to me, and I'll tell you if they are right or not." That is paraphrasing, I guess, paraphrasing the ninth section of the Doctrine and Covenants.

I don't know whom you ought to marry. There are probably ten or fifteen individuals who could qualify. The Lord expects us to do our homework—dating, courting, and so on—make a decision, and then take that decision to him for confirmation.

I don't know what you ought to select as a career in this life. I'm not sure it matters to the Lord. You could do any one of a number of things. But he expects you and me to think about it, and ponder it, and study it, and pray about it. The point is that by developing a personal relationship with our Heavenly Father we can find the solutions to our problems and concerns.

I want you to know, as you face the future, that the Lord hasn't left you alone. There are those who have been placed in our midst who know with certainty the truth of these principles. May we continue to seek so that we may find.

In Self

2

Thinking Big— Dare to Try

William Shakespeare gave us some great wisdom and excellent counsel. Perhaps none was greater than his expression, "Our doubts are traitors and make us lose the good we oft might win by fearing to attempt."

Let me repeat that one more time: "Our doubts are traitors and make us lose the good we oft might win by fearing to attempt." I think most failures are not due to a lack of opportunity but rather to unwillingness to "think big." Sometimes we just do not *dare to try*.

I recall a group of teenage youth in Uruguay who, more out of nerve than talent, entered a soccer tournament. What they lacked in ability they made up for in sheer determination. They had practiced together long and hard, and somehow or other they managed to make it to the championship game. They were obviously outclassed by the defending champions. Unfortunately, someone told them that and they believed it. At the end of the first half the score stood 4-0. They were zero—in more ways than one.

Their coach pulled them aside during half-time. He kept it simple. "Look, you guys, I know what you're up against. I know those guys have talent. But I know you, and let me tell you something. I know you can still win this thing if you really want to. I'm only ashamed because you haven't tried. All I ask is that you go out there and give it your all. I know you guys well enough to know that you have what it takes. Now go do it!" And they did, winning 5 to 4, scoring the final goal in the closing seconds of play as bedlam erupted in the stands. Those young men learned a lesson that will last them a long time.

I recall a young man in Los Angeles who wanted to be an opera star. Several teachers told him that it would do him no good to try because, they said, "You just don't have the voice." But, unwilling to give up, he finally discovered one teacher who saw the value of his hidden talent and big determination. Today, after years of conscientiously and carefully directing his power toward a single goal, he is one of the most pleasing and highly honored singers on the West Coast.

Did you know that Verdi, the composer of some of our finest grand operas, was at one time refused admission to a music conservatory because of his apparent lack of natural ability; and that a prominent music teacher once refused to take Caruso as a student because he could see no musical promise in Caruso's voice?

Just as with those young soccer players in Uruguay, it's not so much a matter of talent as it is determination and willingness to try—to think big. As one good wife recently reminded her husband on a note taped to his bathroom mirror:

> It doesn't take a muscle spasm
> to show a little enthusiasm.

When I wanted to be a ball player some years ago, a great high school coach taught me a valuable principle. When I went in to sign up as a freshman, he asked, "Do you want to be a ball player or a champion?"

I replied, "I want to play ball."

He said, "If you just want to play ball, then you won't play here. But if you want to be a champion, you came to the right place, because I make champions and a champion you will be." Isn't that a great thought!

Now, if you think back with me for a moment on the stories I have just related, you will notice a couple of common threads running through each of them. Once there was a vision of what could be accomplished and an attitude of "I can do it," another critical commitment was made. Besides a willingness to try, there came consciousness of and determination to pay the necessary price.

The Savior advised us to take personal inventory before beginning our task:

"For which of you, intending to build a tower, sitteth not down first, and counteth the cost, whether he have sufficient to finish it?

"Lest haply, after he hath laid the foundation, and is not able to finish it, all that behold it begin to mock him,

"Saying, This man began to build, and was not able to finish." (Luke 14:28—30.)

Some of us, however, being mortals, are willing to consider the cost and make the commitment but just can't seem to follow through. If you're willing to put what I'm talking about to the test, you will find that the Savior was serious when he said:

"There is a law, irrevocably decreed in heaven before the foundations of this world, upon which all blessings are predicated—

"And when we obtain any blessing from God, it is by obedience to that law upon which it is predicated." (D&C 130:20–21.)

The Savior means it. If you're willing to pay the price and do what is necessary, in righteousness, you will certainly reap the reward.

Given an average grade of intelligence, wise direction, and willingness to pay the price of concentrated and consecrated effort—not once a week but constantly, every day of every year—we will find that the secrets of life have a way of revealing themselves beyond our fondest dreams. Most of us know of many cases of particular individuals who years ago were just average or less, but who were not satisfied with mediocrity or being average, and who today exhibit great personal talent. By aligning themselves with great causes, seeking out people who are geniuses in their fields of interest, and training and disciplining themselves, they have gone on to make tremendous contributions to themselves and to society.

Just remember that there will be times of discouragement. But I would encourage you to remember in such times the words of a great coach: "Just remember that when you see a man on top of a mountain he didn't fall there." Success and greatness are processes of climbing, and climb we must.

Life can be exciting. Each one of us should dream, we should think big, we should dare to try. It has been my experience that those who are truly happy in life are those who do. You and I can join those happy people. The Savior of this world has promised his help if we seek it—if our dreams are worthy, if our efforts are to bless those around us. I challenge you—I challenge you to dare to try!

3

Happiness
Is Within You

Where is happiness? For each of us that question forms the basis of a continual quest, doesn't it? No one deliberately seeks sorrow, tragedy, or pain. And yet, in our search for happiness, many of us find ourselves further and further from that joy-producing goal. Why is this? Do we make our odyssey in such darkness that we can't see which way to turn? Or could it be we don't even know what happiness is?

I once asked a special group of ladies what it takes to be happy. Their responses were intriguing:

Young Lady: I could never be happy until I find the right young man and get married.

Somewhat Older Lady: I will never be happy as long as I am married to my husband.

Another Middle-aged Woman: I thought I was miserable before, but now that I'm divorced life is just one big dead end.

Another Woman: My first marriage was beautiful compared to the one I've gotten myself into now.

What these ladies had to say was very interesting, wasn't it? Did you notice what the four of them had in common? I noticed two things. First, they were all unhappy, and second, their hope for future happiness was dependent upon a drastic change in their circumstances. Yes, I would agree with them—their plights are most unfortunate.

There was another thing these four ladies had in common. Each one was unhappy in the exact situation that the previous one had predicted would solve her problem and make her happy. It seems to me, therefore, that happiness is not an outgrowth of desirable circumstance. No, our search must take us in a different direction. Let's look again.

I asked yet another lady about being happy and she said: "Oh, yes, of course I'm happy. I often wonder how I could be happier." I asked what had happened to her that had made her so happy and she responded: "What has happened to me? Does something have to *happen* to me? I was happy yesterday and I expect to be happy tomorrow, too. If I had to wait for something special or different to happen to me before I could be happy, then life would be miserable. But to me, happiness is mine for the taking. All I have to do is live the way I know I should, and then happiness just seems to follow me around and pounce all over me."

What a wise young lady! I think she has discovered the true key to happiness. Happiness does not lie in things or circumstances, but rather in attitudes and applying correct principles in one's life. Having the right attitude is vital. I have participated in athletics most of my life. In games, both important and sandlot, I have seen players become angry because of some circumstance, such as a bad judgment on the part of an umpire or referee, that developed during the game. Then an interesting thing sometimes happened. As the game progressed, the team of the angry player would prove superior and ultimately win the game. Still, the angry player would remain angry, and instead of the victory bringing him happiness it brought him at best a measure of revenge. At worst, it left him still angry and seeking even greater revenge.

Oh, Satan is a crafty one. He uses happiness as the carrot after which the rabbits of humanity run. Little do they realize that the carrot is attached to a string, which is tied to a stick, which is attached to their own back, and no matter how hard they run they will never obtain it. They fail to realize that happiness and true satisfaction are not contained within the carrot, but if found at all must be found within themselves.

The scriptures record that the devil "seeketh that all men might be miserable like unto himself" (2 Nephi 2:27). How foolish the person is who will be trapped by someone as obviously short on intelligence as the devil. Can you imagine giving up the love and glory of God to become the evil one? That is what the devil did, and he went further: he made it his objective to destroy the happiness of all mankind. For being not too smart, he has revealed not his own stupidity but our own.

Let's look in the right place for happiness and for the joy that true happiness will lead us to. Let's look within ourselves. Then, regardless of our circumstance, be it pleasant or unpleasant, we can be happy. Though Gethsemane was the place that brought Jesus his greatest pain and suffering in mortality, it was no doubt also the place that ultimately brought him his greatest happiness. For he found his greatest happiness within himself as he sought to love and serve others. Pain and sorrow had little to do with whether he was happy. And to paraphrase one of his classic statements, we ought to go and do likewise.

4

Shifting the Blame

Sometimes it seems that it is just human nature to shift the blame for our wrongdoings to somebody else. Adam started it. You remember that when the Lord came to him in the garden and asked him if he had eaten of the forbidden fruit, Adam had a ready answer. He didn't say, "It was me. I did it." Instead he blamed Eve for his misconduct: "The woman whom thou gavest to be with me, she gave me of the tree, and I did eat" (Genesis 3:12).

And Eve was no better. When the Lord asked her about the fruit, she answered, "The serpent beguiled me, and I did eat" (Genesis 3:13).

Shifting blame to somebody else did not stop there. When Moses was delayed on the mount while talking to the Lord, the Israelites became restless. When he returned he saw that they were worshipping idols and engaging in a number of sinful practices. Moses turned to Aaron and said, essentially, "What did this people do to you that you should have brought so great a sin upon them?" And Aaron, probably feeling extremely uncomfortable in that awful moment, finally found his answer. He said, "[Don't get angry with me.] Thou knowest the people, that they are set on mischief" (Exodus 32:19—23).

Excuses for our misconduct. We've got a million of them. In the most terrible and shameful moment of history, when the mob was shouting to crucify an innocent man, even the Lord himself, Pontius Pilate found his excuse. He could find no legitimate reason to sentence Jesus to death, but weakly assenting to the crowd, he washed his hands, saying, "I am innocent of the blood of this just person" (Matthew 27:24).

Today, we have an interesting twist on this old theme of shifting the blame. When people murder, mug, or traffic in drugs, we blame society. There is no such thing as personal responsibility. Rather, a society that allows poverty and violence is all to blame.

But amidst all this refusal to own up to one's own misconduct, there are yet those who typify the words on a sign that used to sit on Harry Truman's desk. It said simply, "The buck stops here." In a world where people commonly shift blame to others and deny responsibility for things as they are, how refreshing is that little message, "The buck stops here."

There was once a young man who did not get that message. It seems that at the age of seventeen he began to run with a gang of boys. They had great fun together and he always looked forward to being with them. One night after they had been together, he left them and went home to bed. After some time he heard a great noise that seemed to come from the shouting and yelling of excited people. Being curious, he dressed and went downstairs. He was right. It was a mob, and to his surprise, it seemed to be coming toward his house. It was not long before it arrived; from it sprang three or four of his friends, all members of the gang. One of them said to him, "Come with us, Joe! This guy we have has molested a girl and we're going to lynch him!" Before he could ask any questions, they grabbed him by the arms and he was swept along with this swirling, shouting sea of people.

A mile from his house was a large oak tree. Almost before he knew what was happening, they arrived at that tree. Quickly they placed a rope around the man's neck, placed him on a horse, and threw the rope over the limb of the tree. The moment of death had arrived.

Suddenly a profound silence came over the mob. All but one last detail for the lynching had been completed. Quite by chance, our young man found himself right next to the horse. Suddenly the leader—and every mob has such a leader—shouted at him, "Joe, kick that horse and let's get this thing over with." There he was with all those people watching him and anxious for him to carry out the command. He felt the beating hearts—his own and all the rest—responding to this moment of tragic urgency. He hesitated, but then blinded by emotion and the desire to have the approval of the mob, he kicked the horse. The man met his death.

The next day, the group discovered that they had lynched an innocent human being. This man had had nothing to do with the alleged crime. And so what if he had been guilty? No one should ever meet such a death at the hands of a senseless mob.

Now, our man involved said this: "For sixty-five years I have tried to find peace. I have wished in the agony of my soul that at that moment when the mob took me with them and I found myself by the side of that horse, I had had the ability and courage to live my life as my conscience dictated." But he hadn't. And he spent a lifetime of being haunted for that one moment when he had refused personal responsibility for the events. For that one moment, he could almost believe that the mob had made him do it. But a lifetime of personal torment had taught him better. He couldn't shift the blame for the night's activities to someone else. In the crucible of crowd pressure, he had succumbed. (Experience related to Reed Bradford.)

Now, the question that is left to us is this: "Are we daring enough to take the personal responsibility for our actions and the quality of our hearts? Or are we always looking for an excuse to explain away what we are?" You've all heard comments like these: "I would have done it, but . . ." or "You never make me happy," or "It might have been." All these are subtle ways of saying, in effect, "I'm not responsible."

But let's face it squarely. You are responsible for who you are. You are responsible for what you do. And someday you will have to report to the Lord on what you have done with your life. It won't be enough in that day to say, "Everybody was doing it," or "Everybody thought that." You are responsible for you.

I have a great friendship with a man who learned this lesson early in his youth. He discovered the importance of doing what is right regardless of peer pressure. He has been kind enough to put into writing an experience that changed his life. I share his insight in his own words.

"I was in the ninth grade. A year in which it seemed I was halfway to nowhere. Confidence was not part of my nature. My actions were largely controlled by my feelings of inferiority.

"During third period I sat near the back of the classroom. My feet extended as far forward as I could stretch them. By sitting in this manner I was scarcely visible from where the teacher sat at her desk in the front.

"Friday was the day for current events. When the roll was called, each student had two choices—he could either answer 'prepared' or 'unprepared.' If his response was 'unprepared' he didn't have to do anything. I quickly grasped the idea that the word 'unprepared' was the word that would get me off the hook.

"As the weeks went by, each time my name was called I responded almost with dignity, 'unprepared.' My friends also mastered this word. We all, as a group, made it easier for each of us as individuals.

"A girl that I liked very much sat in front of me. I liked her so much that on the way to school I would think of clever things to say to her, but when in her presence, my mind would go blank and I would become almost tongue-tied.

"One day when the teacher called the roll and got to my name, I replied, 'Unprepared.' It was then that this girl did me a great favor. She turned around, looked back at me, and said, 'Why don't you get prepared?' I was not able to listen to any of the reports that day. I kept thinking of all sorts of wonderful things like, 'What does she care, unless she cares?'

"I went home, found an article in the newspaper, and read it time and again until I had finally committed it to memory. I cut the article out, folded it, placed it in my wallet, and carried it with me all week.

"The next Friday I was there in my usual seat in the back. The teacher started to call the roll without looking up. Finally she got to my name; she said 'George?' and very quietly I gave a great speech—I said, 'Prepared.'

"She stopped calling the roll and looked up at me. I poked my head up as far as I could and nodded. The girl turned around and smiled. My friends looked over at me like, 'Traitor!' Then I sat waiting my turn, saying to myself, 'What have I done?' I was scared. Then I made a magnificent discovery. It was all right to be afraid if I didn't let it stop me from doing what I should.

"My turn came. I went to the front and started to speak. I remembered every word, and after the last word had crossed my lips, I stood there for just a second, and a priceless thought passed my mind and found its way to my heart. I said to myself, 'I like you!'

"I returned to my seat and sat down. I didn't hear any of the reports, but as my heart pounded within me, I kept feeling over and over again, 'This is the only way to live.'

"I have since learned that the word 'unprepared' really does take you off the hook and lead you away from pressure. By learning to say that word you really don't have to do anything, but you never know the joy of doing something that causes you to say to yourself, 'I like myself.' " (George Durrant, *The New Era*, Jan-Feb, 1981, p. 39.)

Make no mistake. Your soul is in your own hands. No one makes you do anything. And the standard by which we should guide our lives is simply this: "How would the Savior behave in this situation?" May we always have the power to do right in the face of pressure.

5

Don't Do It!

Over the years I have counseled with young and old, male and female, married and unmarried. People with problems have told me of their sorrow, their regret. It has been interesting to listen to those who have succumbed to transgressions. It has also been tragic. But through those countless interviews, I have heard the same phrases repeated over and over; phrases of justifications for acts that most often have resulted in hurtful, serious consequences. Here are a few:

Don't be chicken.
Just once won't hurt.
Everyone else is doing it.
No one will ever know.
That's the way the ball bounces, so let it happen.
Enjoy it while you can.
You only live once.

The list goes on and on, and so do the transgressions.

Then there comes another set of phrases. These are more sober, more sorrowful. They go something like this:

I wish it were yesterday.
I wish I hadn't said it.
I wish I hadn't done it.
If only I had listened.
Why did I have to be so foolish?
If I only had one more chance.

This list also goes on and on. The only difference is that the list becomes more somber and, at times, almost unbearable.

Have you noticed that temptation is all around us? You would have to be almost dead not to notice. Satan is alive and well, and is more clever than ever before. He loves to see us unhappy. He rejoices in our wrong doings. He wants us to be as miserable as he is, and I have noticed that we accommodate him all too often. We play around with sin as if we have the power to do so and not be hurt.

There is a story of a cobra which a man from the Far East had trained. Back and forth, back and forth, the cobra's head moved in rhythm with the exotic music the man played. Then one day there was a crashing sound, and the little man fell helplessly to the ground. He had carelessly tempted the cobra once too often, and so it is with sin.

I love sports and I can hold my own in several. Basketball is not one of them. I never could do too well going one-on-one. Now, I may be slow, but I am not dumb. I know better than to go one-on-one with someone of greater skill. There are too many lunches to buy when you do that sort of thing. But somehow, we think we can go one-on-one with Satan. It won't work and it never has. He is too skilled and the price is too high. Nevertheless, there are plenty of us who are always looking for a pick-up game with temptation. We don't want to avoid it at all.

It's like this story I heard recently. A man consulted a doctor. "I've been misbehaving, doc, and my conscience is troubling me," he complained. "And you want something that will strengthen your willpower?" asked the doctor. "Well, no," said the fellow, "I was thinking of something that would weaken my conscience."

We have all felt that kind of desire on occasion. Happily, many have resisted—unhappily, some haven't. May I give some counsel regarding transgressions and the temptation to indulge? It comes not only from my observations, but also from my experience.

You and I need to try harder to avoid the very appearance of evil. I admit it isn't easy, but it is easier than the alternative.

I have a friend who is a teacher, and a good one. He recently told me the following story, which is just the thing to demonstrate my point:

"On one occasion, I was to teach a lesson on the dangers of sin and temptation. A friend of mine indicated an approach he used in such a situation. He gathered a number of different traps to use in his demonstration. One was a small mouse trap, then a larger rat trap, followed by a muskrat trap, and then a coyote trap. If possible, he would borrow a bear trap for effect. Then he would set the traps, talk to his students about temptation and sin, and one by one trigger each trap as the degree of sin went up. The mouse trap he would set off with his own finger, allowing himself to be slapped by the trap. Then he would use a ruler or a small stick to trigger the other traps, often breaking the stick in the process.

"I was interested in doing a similar thing with my students. My friend agreed to loan me the needed traps and to explain how they worked. As arranged, one Saturday we met to discuss the proper approach to this lesson. He had brought along his four-year-old daughter to keep him company. We proceeded to set the traps, learn how to set them off, and in the process we talked and laughed about the fun of setting the traps and relating them to various sins and temptations. We played with the trigger mechanisms, laughing and challenging each other relative to each trap. All of this was intended to create the excitement and thrill of danger involved with the perception of sin. At that point we sat down to discuss the proper strategy in making this presentation lively for the students.

"Unknown to us, my friend's daughter had been watching us from a distance. She wanted to be part of the fun, and when we sat down to talk, she took the opportunity to see just how fun it really was. We didn't see her until her hand was raised over the coyote trap. As her hand began moving downward, the two of us flew into action. My friend grabbed for his daughter and I dove with both hands for the trap. The timing couldn't have been more perfect. She had already triggered the trap, but at precisely that instant I was able to stop the upward motion of the jaws and my friend was able to extract her hand from danger. We then sat down, both of us terribly shaken by the nearness of tragedy."

Do you see how just the very appearance of sin can cause problems? Even innocent bystanders can be hurt. The Lord wasn't kidding when he said: "Watch and pray, that ye enter not into temptation" (Matthew 26:41). May we be so fortunate.

My last little bit of counsel concerns the challenge of meeting temptation straight on. We can't avoid the confrontation, but what we do about it is up to us.

May I suggest two plans of attack. First, we should make up our minds that we simply won't give in to temptation. Making up our minds is half the battle. That solution may sound over-simplified, but I know of no other way. So, since there is no way around it, why don't we decide *right now* that we won't give in? That kind of commitment won't guarantee that we won't sin, but it surely will help prevent us from committing many of the more serious offenses. Eventually, that kind of determination will lead us to repeat the words of Plato: "If I were sure God would pardon me, and men would not know my sin, yet I should be ashamed to sin because of its essential baseness."

Wouldn't it be great if we could get to that point? We can, but only if we begin right now with a resolve to do better. It will take a lifetime to complete, but the sooner we start, the better we will be.

Second, we should remember the counsel of the Apostle Paul in advising us that temptation is common to us all. He also reassured us that when we are tempted, a loving Father "will with the temptation also make a way to escape, that ye may be able to bear it" (1 Corinthians 10:13). I believe that! I have seen that promise fulfilled too many times to deny it.

So, I suggest that when we are tempted, we remember Paul's advice and turn to the Lord. He can help. He will help if we will humble ourselves and ask. When we're tempted to betray ourselves and our families for instant gratification, it is my experience that God will help if we will seek him. He wants to do so. He waits anxiously to do so. May we take him at his word. We'll be a lot happier if we do, of that I assure you.

6

Graduation Gowns

I recently participated in the graduation proces-
sional at an esteemed university. I watched as men and
women, young and old, received their diplomas. The
recipients came in all sizes, shapes, and colors. They
were religious, nonreligious, politically active, and politically inactive. They were brilliant and average (whatever
that is). They were everything! About the only things
these educated men and women had in common were
their graduation caps and gowns. They were all basically
the same color and design.

I have pondered the sight of those fifteen hundred
graduates. They looked educated and they acted educated, at least until after the commencement was over.
The diplomas they received implied that they were
educated. But I wonder, were they really? Which ones?

What's the difference? What is education and who is really educated?

I feel perfectly justified in letting the world know I received my doctorate from a great university. I have my diploma. That *proves* I'm educated. If I don't *act* educated it's all right, because I have my certificate. Once you have a diploma, no one can dispute your claim to education.

Well, we all know that a diploma doesn't prove anything except that we have an attractive piece of paper and have at least been through the motions. But I believe that just as everyone who graduated that day wore a graduation cap and gown, there are also some common elements in the truly educated man and woman. There is a common covering for the educated.

Allow me to describe at least a few characteristics of the covering of an educated person. It isn't complete, but it will get us started. This series of characteristics is brought to us from a compilation of comments of those who consider themselves educated. It applies to both men and women. Here we go:

1. An educated man listens as his son reads the latest Dick and Jane book to him.

2. An educated man is an investor who picks up the business section of the newspaper first and reads the jokes.

3. An educated man is one who says nothing when there is nothing to say.

4. An educated man is one who says, "That's the best burnt roast I've ever had."

5. An educated man wears his battle scars gracefully.

6. An educated man laughs when the joke is on him.

7. An educated man is one who gets another man to do his heavy work.

8. An educated man gets as big a thrill from his two-year-old proclaiming, "Daddy, I love you!" as he does from finding that the stock he bought last week has gone up five points.

9. An educated man listens to others, and then thinks for himself.

10. An educated man decides to swim rather than sink.

11. An educated man can put a toy together without his son's help.

12. An educated man's library gets bigger and his golf score gets smaller.

13. An educated man asks "Why?" when others don't care.

14. An educated man will laugh when his friend tells a joke he has heard before.

15. An educated man is a man who can reach for the sky, yet have his feet on solid ground.

16. An educated man is rare.

17. An educated man can be *any* man. (Author unidentified.)

Now, put your diploma up against that! I scored myself as I read those characteristics. I won't tell you how I did, but while my library *does* get larger, my golf score is another matter. As I recall it, "An educated man does not reveal his golf score." Even Jack Nicklaus has his problems. Jack once made this statement:

"When I make a mistake on the golf course I like to know why. Was my alignment poor, my grip bad, my hand position wrong? Did I take the club away too fast?

Did I pick the club up, did I take it to the outside, did I take it to the inside, did I sway? Did I move over the top with my right shoulder? Did I move my head? There are a million things . . . ; quite often I'll find my mistake. All I have to do is to find it once or twice during a round and I won't repeat it again." (*Travel Leisure*, April–May, 1971.)

I'm not sure what kind of diploma Jack has, but he sounds educated to me. In fact, Jack *is* educated. I have watched him many times and I can vouch for his education—in the real sense of that word.

There are plenty of educated golfers in the world. At least there are if we accept Robert Frost's definition of education. He once defined education as "the ability to listen to almost anything without losing your temper or self-confidence" (Johann Schiller, *The Home Book of Quotations*, p. 1119). By that same definition, there are some uneducated golfers, as there are teachers, plumbers, bankers, lawyers, housewives and cab drivers. The ability to confront an issue or a person without losing your cool is one mark of truly educated people. It's part of their covering.

Let me mention another part of the "graduation gown" of an educated man. It is his ability to look, to learn, and to do better. I think it's a pretty well accepted fact that we learn 80% with our eyes, 18% with our ears, and 2% with whatever else. Well, if that's true, and if we are going to be educated, we need to keep our eyes open and pay attention. I know a university professor or two who would do well to remember that. When we don't look, we don't learn. But when we do, great things happen. Our desire to do better increases. I saw printed on the side of a milk truck these words: "Our cows are not contented, they're anxious to do better." So is an educated man.

Remember there is another element of education that is vital. I was reminded of it as I read this brief description of an educated man by Roy L. Smith. He describes pretty well what an educated man is like:

"He finds more of life's wealth in the common pleasures—home, health, children.

"He thinks more about the worth of men and less about their wealth.

"He begins to appreciate his own father a little more.

"He boasts less and boosts more.

"He hurries less, and usually makes more progress.

"He esteems the friendship of God a little higher."

It is with a discussion about that last quality that I wish to conclude. The friendship of God is a vital covering of the educated man. I have found that those who are really, truly educated are in the process of coming to know their God. And, not surprisingly, they are in the process of understanding who they really are.

A story is told of the son of King Louis XVI of France. As a young man, he was abducted by the same evil men who had dethroned the king. These men sought to destroy the son in every way. He was subjected to every conceivable kind of filth. He was exposed to vile men and lewd women. He saw and heard what no man should see or hear. But he would not buckle under the pressure. Those who sought to destroy him morally were confounded. In their search for an answer to his moral strength he provided this comment: "I cannot do what you ask, for I was born to be a king."

Every man and woman is born to be a king or queen. If we are truly educated, we will sense that truth even while learning it. We are all children of God. The educated are in the process of making that discovery.

That about sums it up. As I have observed it, education has something to do with classrooms, instructors, and diplomas, but those ingredients by themselves aren't sufficient. The graduation gown of an educated person represents much more than that. A formal education can help—but it can also hinder.

May you and I both seek to become educated. It will be an eternal process, but one worth pursuing. And as we seek that education, let's remember who we are. The world is in desperate need of educated people, with or without a diploma.

That we may don the covering of the truly educated is my hope for us all.

7

To Try

I love good music. I won't define the term "good music" because I have had teenagers and I realize that tastes vary, especially between children and parents. It's surprising how much my former teenagers and I now agree on what constitutes good music. I wonder who changed?

Well, the other evening I was listening to some good music and happened to hear the song "The Impossible Dream." It was a good listening experience, and as I listened, one line in particular stood out from the rest: "To try when your arms are too weary." Trying when your arms are too weary has to be one of life's greatest challenges. I suppose those words stood out for me because of an account I read recently of a young woman athlete. I thought it most inspirational.

The incident took place in New York City at the 1982 running of the marathon. More than 15,000 runners began the race; after seven hours, more than 13,500 had finished. Soon, it began to get dark, but the race wasn't over for one young woman. Linda Downs was determined to finish the race. You see, Linda Downs had been born with cerebral palsy and was running the course on crutches.

She had to make her way carefully because of all the litter left in the wake of the race. She fell six times, but six times she got back up and continued on her way.

Soon the news media caught wind of what Linda was doing. Two-thirds of the way to the finish line, only her family and a few friends were there to cheer her on. But others quickly joined their ranks. Strangers cheered and called out their support. Eleven hours after she began, Linda Downs crossed the finish line.

People from throughout the country wrote her letters. Media people applauded her efforts long and loud. Even President Reagan invited her to lunch at the White House.

But the story does not end there. In 1983, Linda again entered the New York City marathon and improved her time by almost two hours.

What an amazing feat! But not only is it amazing, it is realistic. That's right, it's realistic. There are Linda Downses all over this world, people who make it through the most difficult circumstances, who continue to try when their arms are too weary.

Calvin Coolidge once made a statement that accurately describes people like Linda Downs. He said: "Nothing in this world can take the place of persistence.

Talent will not; nothing is more common than unsuccessful men with talent. Genius will not; unrewarded genius is almost a proverb. Education will not; the world is full of educated derelicts. Persistence and determination alone are omnipotent. The slogan 'press on' has solved and always will solve the problems of the human race." If ever a truth was uttered, that is one. Going on when things are tough is an ability that any one of us can develop. I don't know who said it, but someone observed that "When the going gets tough, the tough get going."

A reporter was interviewing an old gentleman on his hundredth birthday. "To what do you attribute your longevity?" he asked.

The old man thought for a moment, then replied, "I never smoked, I never drank liquor, I never fooled around with women, and I always got up at six every morning."

The reporter duly noted the old man's formula, then commented, "I had an uncle who did the same thing, but he only lived to eighty. How do you account for that?"

"Simple," said the old man. "He didn't keep at it long enough."

Well, there it is! There is one of life's great secrets. We must learn to keep at it long enough. If we do, the results can astound us.

Persistence is a great attitude to have. It will not only keep us encouraged, it will discourage those who attempt to block our way. Being a history buff, I remember the story of the handful of Spartans who held a mountain pass against hundreds of Persians. The odds were overwhelming. The Persians tried unsuccessfully to get the Spartans to surrender. They finally sent emissaries to talk to the Spartans. They hoped to persuade the Spartans to surrender by making the ultimate threat. The Persians said, "We have so many archers in our army that we can darken the skies with our arrows." And then came the classic reply of the Spartans. In the same spirit as Linda Downs and Calvin Coolidge, they said: "So much the better; we shall fight in the shade." I love their spunk, their persistence. It's impossible to beat someone who won't be beaten.

There is an eight-line poem that sums up our challenge. It has no title and I do not know who the author is, but whoever wrote it understood what we're talking about.

> Stick to your task until it sticks to you;
> Beginners are many, but enders are few.
> Honor, power, place, and praise
> Will always come to the one who stays.
>
> Stick to your task until it sticks to you;
> Bend at it, sweat at it, smile at it, too;
> For out of the bend, and the sweat, and the smile
> Will come life's victories after a while.

I am convinced that the "after a while" part of the poem will eventually come, even though it may seem as if it never will. I think we all have a common tendency: When things go wrong, we are sure that they will never end. But I assure you that they will. But don't get the mistaken idea that things are going to go smoothly for too long. If I remember correctly, the "law of life's highway," goes something like this: "If everything is coming your way, You're in the wrong lane" (Arthur Block,

Murphy's Law: Book II). And the way life really is, you don't drive in the wrong lane very long before switching back. At least you don't if you want to survive.

The courage to try even when we think we're too tired is one of the most rewarding of life's experiences. Any runner knows that if he persists, he will eventually get his second wind. And when that occurs, there is a feeling of exhilaration that is almost indescribable. We sometimes cheat ourselves of such a feeling by giving up too soon.

And finally, speaking of runners, the Apostle Paul speaks of his own race. At the conclusion of his life, he made this critical analysis of his mission: "I have fought a good fight, I have finished my course, I have kept the faith" (2 Timothy 4:7). We can do the same thing. Whether it's maintaining our virtue, our honesty, or our integrity; whether it's fighting an illness or physical handicap; whether it's overcoming the discouragement of a disastrous marriage or terrible home life; whether it's simply "hanging in there" during our days of discouragement and depression, we can do it! I am absolutely sure of that. I see people all around me who do. If they can do it, so can we.

May we turn to Him who can fortify us. The Lord has strength sufficient for us all. We all have quiet moments when we wonder if we will survive. I firmly believe that we will. If we will but persist, if we will try when we think we cannot go on, he will pull us through, of that I am sure.

8

Stronger Than Medicine

Let me begin by telling you the story of a father and son. It's not a typical father-son story, and maybe that's one of the interesting things about it:

An aging father had a business that he knew would eventually go to his son. The father desired to take things easier, so he announced that if his son could bring him five hundred dollars that he had earned himself (something the son had never done before), the business would be his from that moment on.

The mother of the boy decided to help her son (as she had always done). So quietly she gave him five hundred dollars and told him to dress in the clothes of a laborer when he brought the money to his father.

"Here, father," said the boy, "here is the five hundred dollars that I have made myself."

The father took the money and, without looking up from his evening paper, tossed the money into the fireplace where it was consumed by the fire.

"Son," said the mother later, "you weren't convincing —and you've got to be convincing around your father. Now here's another five hundred dollars. Try it again."

This time the son made sure that he had dirtied up his clothes and his hands and then appeared physically tired when he came to his father with the money.

The father did the same as before. Without looking up from his paper, he threw the five hundred dollars on the fire while the son watched, horrified.

With this turn of events, the son decided that perhaps he had better go out and really make the five hundred dollars. His father, he realized, would be convinced in no other way. At long last he came to his father with another five hundred dollars.

But again the father, without looking up, threw the money into the fireplace.

Instantly, the son reached into the flames without regard for his own safety or the pain of the burning flesh, and pulled back the money.

"Son," the father said, looking up from the paper, "I see that you've earned *that* money."

Now, for five hundred dollars, I think I may have put my hand in the fire the first time. I'm quite certain I would have the second time. A thousand dollars is a thousand dollars. May I ask you what it would take to get you to put your hand in the fire? Money? Prestige? Power? Fame? Love?

Whatever the motivation, we won't do anything until our desire is strong enough. Desire is an awesome power.

If a man or woman has a strong enough desire, he or she can accomplish almost anything.

I recall my early romance and courtship with my wife —once she got it into her beautiful head that I was the one for her, her desire did the rest. I didn't have a chance. I finally accepted her proposal because she wouldn't take no for an answer. Before you believe that, let me assure you that, in fact, I did the pursuing and she did the accepting. But strong desire did enter in.

It's interesting to see what motivates people, what gives them their desire. It's not always the same. If the desire isn't really kindled, nothing happens. Permit me to illustrate.

A prominent minister some years ago arrived in a small town to preach a sermon. Wanting to mail a letter, he asked a young boy where the post office was. When the boy had told him, the minister thanked him and said, "If you'll come to the church this evening, you can hear me tell everyone how to get to heaven."

"What's the good of coming to hear you?" the boy said. "You don't even know your way to the post office."

Someone who doesn't know where he's going won't have the power to motivate anyone. Whether you're the president, the prime minister, or an executive, you will only do something when you have a strong desire.

Here's another story to demonstrate the point. I don't know if it's true or not, but if it isn't it should be.

A minister, his spirits low, went into the sanctuary to pray. Falling to his knees, he lamented, "Oh, Lord, I am nothing! I am nothing!"

The assistant minister happened by, and overcome by the humility of the minister, dropped to his knees beside the other. Shortly he, too, was crying out, "Oh, Lord, I, too, am nothing, nothing!"

The janitor of the church, awed by the sight of the two men praying, joined them, moaning, "Oh, Lord, I also am nothing! I am nothing, nothing!"

At this the assistant minister nudged the minister and said, "Now look who thinks he's nothing!"

It is impossible to overestimate the influence of others on our own personal desires. Teenagers are a great example. They love to be in style, and rightly so. Their desire for the latest fashions stems from watching others. If one kneels at the altar of fashion, another one comes and kneels with him. If two are better, three is even more so, and the more the merrier. Our desires are kindled by the world around us.

I propose, however, that before we allow ourselves to be pushed by those around us, we should take a second look at our desires and make sure they're right. We can verify them by going to a much wiser source. I refer, of course, to our Heavenly Father. Before we let our strong desire get away from us, a calm conversation with Deity can help us know for certain that our desires are not misplaced. However, even then we must use some common sense. A young man at a local university shared the following experience:

"When I was a young boy, at the age of six, I received a brace in my teeth which came loose after eating some candy.

"One day as I was creating my own mud pools, my brace fell out in the water. I searched for about 45 minutes, then the words from Mother and all the Sunday School teachers came back. 'If you ever get into trouble or need help, call on your Father in Heaven.' So I did and still never found the brace.

"When I was twelve or so I entered a Pentathalon. I was in the high jump finals. So I said, 'Okay, Lord, here's your second chance.' I knocked the pole over both times. Then I remembered what I used to do when Mother would come in for prayers at night. This one night I had written the prayer out and taped it on the wall. Mother came in and said how proud she was that I had written my prayer on the wall. She waited for me to say my prayers, and I just sat there. She said, 'Aren't you going to say your prayers tonight?' I said, 'Well, if God's up there, he can read it.'

"He always seems to answer our prayers in the way we need it. I never needed that brace after that because all my teeth are in my mouth, and the high jump wasn't going to affect my eternal salvation in the long run anyway." (Mark Clark, Brigham Young University, 1971.)

The cold, hard fact is that a wise heavenly parent doesn't always have the same desire that we do. I have seen my own children struggle with that one, as most of us have. It's tough to deal with. But before we allow our strong desires to carry us away, we need to know if *our desires* are *his*. If they are, nothing can stop us. Some examples come to mind:

1. Peter's desire to take the gospel to the Gentiles was also the Lord's idea.

2. Paul's desire to preach in Rome originated with the Lord.

3. John's desire to share the visions of Patmos was inspired by Deity.

The list could go on and on; the exciting thing to me

is that the same heavenly motivation is being manifested in the desires of thousands of great people in our day. Such a man is Earl Bailey:

"Earl Bailey is a man paralyzed from his shoulders to his toes, who taught himself to paint with a brush between his teeth. At the age of three, polio left Earl Bailey without the use of his arms or his legs. At six he learned to write with a pencil in his mouth. At eleven he won a prize in a magazine contest. In his late twenties he held his first exhibit in the living room of his home. All the townspeople attended, and every piece was sold. That was the hour of triumph for a great soul. His paintings have since been hung in almost every museum in Canada. Physicians prize his work most. They find more help for crippled, handicapped patients in one Bailey canvas than in a chestful of medicine." (Bryant S. Hinckley, *Not By Bread Alone* [Salt Lake City: Bookcraft, 1955], p. 98.)

I submit that Earl Bailey's desires are confirmed, if not originated, by a higher source. If they were not, I doubt seriously that they could have been achieved.

Now, one final thought. Once we feel good about our desires, we need to press forward. Righteous desires, no matter how strong, can waver. Even the strongest will can falter. I have seen it in others and I have seen it in myself. Since that is the case, I recommend to us all the words of Sir Winston Churchill. During some of his country's darkest hours, Mr. Churchill uttered these words: "Never give in, never give in, never, never, never, never" (Robert Rhodes James, *Winston S. Churchill: His Complete Speeches*, 6:6, p. 499). That ought to be engraved in every heart.

For those people, especially, who have strong desires to do good, Mr. Churchill's words should be etched in gold. Even at the price of gold, they are more than worth it.

We must formulate in our hearts the best desires, and then have them verified. And we must never give in as we attempt to accomplish them. Whether the desire is to be a better father or mother, daughter or son, brother or sister, let us pursue it with full purpose of heart.

9

Skin Deep

I had to chuckle the other night as I read an oft-quoted statement on beauty. It went something like this: "Beauty is only skin deep, but ugly goes all the way through."

Now, to those of us who would not win a Miss or Mr. America contest, that statement is less than hilarious. But even plain folk understand the point.

Speaking of beauty and those contests to determine who is the most beautiful in the world, I remember vividly a world beauty pageant I watched several years ago. I sat with my family in front of the TV and each of us had picked the one we thought would win. I recall that part of the contest when each contestant was asked to respond to a question. The young lady I had selected was one of the finalists; she was poised and radiant. She was asked the question, and I sat disbelieving as her answer bordered on the obscene. Her response was suggestive and inappropriate. I guess it appealed to the judges, however, because she won. But she also lost, at least to many of us who watched her. She lost, and something also happened to her beauty. She suddenly seemed to lose her glow, her inner self began to show through the outer body, and to my amazement, she no longer seemed beautiful. I'm not sure I can explain what happened, but the exposure of her heart and mind began to fade her good looks. She seemed to be very plain. That experience left an impression on me that I have not forgotten.

Many times since then I have pondered that experience and have carefully tried to analyze the ingredients of real beauty. Having done so, may I suggest that real beauty has very little to do with good looks? I'd like to revise the opening couplet just a little. I will change two words, but they make a world of difference. How about this: "Ugly is only skin deep, but beauty goes all the way through." That makes much more sense to me.

Let me illustrate my point by reminding you of another contest of sorts. It's called the Special Olympics. Have you ever witnessed one? If you get a chance, don't miss it. I have watched several and they are therapy to my soul. Handicapped youngsters compete in every sport imaginable. And when I say compete, that's what I mean. Just sit in the stands and watch the fifty-yard dash and you'll see real beauty. Some of these kids are definitely not physically attractive, but something happens inside when you see some of them struggle down the track. Crooked legs, twisted bodies, damaged minds, wheel chairs, and crutches are all part of those races. And when you see their faces as they cross the finish line, you would have to be a fairly hardened individual to be able to hold back the tears. I can only say I could not. Each one is a winner. Each one gets a hug. Each one gets a medal or ribbon and each one is beautiful. And I am talking about real beauty.

To amplify the concept of real beauty, let me retell a story I have always enjoyed. It's a good example that "beauty goes all the way through."

A New England minister had a fourteen-year-old son. One afternoon the boy's teacher contacted the minister to ask why the boy had not been at school for three days. The minister had no idea; he thought his son had been in class every day.

After some time, the father heard his son coming home, so he met the errant boy at the front door. Immediately the boy knew his father knew about those three days away from school. Together they went into the father's library to discuss what had happened.

The minister explained that he had talked with his son's teacher earlier that day, who had called to see if he was sick. He then told his son how deeply hurt he was to know that he could no longer trust his son.

Knowing how disappointed his father was in him was very hard on the young boy. He would have preferred to be taken to the woodshed than to have broken his father's heart as he had done. But harder yet was when his father asked him to get on his knees so they could pray together for the Lord's forgiveness. As the minister bared his soul before his Maker, the boy realized even more how his conduct had hurt his father. By the time they got up from their knees, both had eyes filled with tears.

The minister knew that his son felt bad, but he also

knew that the boy would have to suffer somewhat for his sin. Therefore, he made up a bed for his son in the attic and told him he would have to stay there for as long as he had been living the lie—three days. His parents would bring him his meals, but he would need to stay in the attic throughout the three days.

After the boy went to the attic, the minister and his wife had a very rough evening. They could think of nothing but their son. They couldn't eat or sleep, although they tried to go through all the motions. Finally, at two o'clock in the morning, the minister rose from his bed and made his way up to the boy's bed in the attic.

The minister and his wife had not been alone in their sleeplessness. Their son, too, had been awake, lying alone in the silence with tears running down his cheeks. Silently, father and son embraced; then the father slipped between the sheets and slept the night with his son.

To me, that is a beautiful story. And to complete the story, the father stayed the next two nights with his son. I don't know what physical good looks that man possessed, but he was beautiful "all the way through."

There is another well-known phrase that bears repeating at this point. Someone once made an observation and put it something like this: "Beauty is in the eye of the beholder."

I believe that to be true. Then, if we add a scripture, we have the whole picture. Our Heavenly Father has given us this truth: "But behold, verily, verily, I say unto you that mine eyes are upon you" (D&C 38:7). I affirm that real beauty is truly in the eye of the beholder. And the very being that created us has his eye on us all. We are all his children. We are all beautiful. At least we can become so if we work at it. As a friend of mine observed, "I haven't met a really ugly human being, but some have come breathtakingly close!" I like his positive attitude.

Let me conclude with a couple of practical suggestions that will improve our looks. We don't need to go to a spa or beautician to do these things. But if we do them consistently, a beauty will shine right through us.

First, why don't we really try looking beyond outward appearances? Check the inner beauty. Look beyond "skin deep." Let's look all the way through. Such a procedure will surprise us. Crooked teeth, extra weight, pimples, warts, and straight hair will all disappear, and we will see beauty as we have never seen it before.

Second, once we begin to look beyond the exterior, let's treat each other as we really should—as sons and daughters of God. Instead of judging someone, let's hold off until we discover what that person is really like. I know some handsome men and lovely women who are as plain as can be on the outside.

I assure you that if we do those two simple things, we'll discover beauty all over the place. And, just as importantly, we will become more beautiful in the eyes of Him who really counts.

In Others

10

Advice, Who Needs It?

I was eating a box of Cracker Jack with one of my grandsons the other day and out of that box came some real wisdom. Sometimes little prizes with printed messages or advice of some kind come inside the box, and would you believe, I got one that said, "He who throws mud loses much ground." Now, that's powerful advice.

We've all been subjected to advice from time to time, some of it good, some bad. Another has said, "It is surprising how many people remember the good advice that they gave, and how few people remember the bad advice they gave," or as one old sage remarked, "Advice is the one thing which is more blessed to give than to receive."

My daughters used to say, "Girls who give advice to others, go to proms with their brothers." Coleridge put it this way: "Advice is like snow: the softer it falls, the longer it dwells upon and the deeper it sinks into the mind."

I remember hearing a speaker say on one occasion, "I realize that giving advice is usually a thankless business, and I assure you that I shall not venture far in that direction." I have always kept in mind the unconsciously profound summation written by a small school girl: "Socrates," she wrote, "was a Greek philosopher who went about giving people good advice. They poisoned him."

What I'm getting at is that it's easy to laugh at cleverly worded gems like the ones I just quoted, but some advice is not easy to take.

Say, for example, that you're seven years old and you're a boy, and your mother tells you to wear your sister's coat to school because you lost yours. Your sister's coat has a big Valentine heart on the front. And remember the time you had your heart broken by your number one love, and your sister said, "I didn't like the way she combed her hair anyway." Now, there's some advice you can hardly wait to step around.

And right after you were married both sets of parents kept reminding you of all the do's and don'ts? Then, one time, when you grew older, you'd just had your heart broken by some disaster, and you were kneeling there by your bed just before going to sleep. The Lord put the thought in your mind that you should leave your burden at his feet. You got up from your knees feeling somewhat helpless and puzzled about what to do next.

Maybe you haven't identified with any of the previous pictures I have tried to paint, but I don't know of a single way a person could make it through life without needing some advice. Some of us get too much and others don't get enough of the right kind, but I believe we all seek good counsel and advice. We all go to some-body.

The person who doesn't seek advice sits alone, tries to make all his own decisions, and tries to become what the world calls "self-sufficient." That term, *self-sufficient*, applies only to weeds in the garden, not to people. I have never met anyone who is truly self-sufficient. Weeds are self-sufficient and weeds always die. Individuals who act and try to be self-sufficient have similar difficulties.

Some years ago, during the Korean War, an army leader tried to act self-sufficient. As a platoon leader he received a communique from his commanding general. It read, "I am sending you and your men to a ridge located at the following map points. You are to arrive at the ridge at precisely 0200 hours and observe the enemy until 0210 hours." That meant he'd have to just sit for ten minutes, looking at the enemy from this secret place high above them. He was directed to descend then with his men into a combat situation at exactly ten minutes after two.

He had received his instructions and advice. He took his men to the ridge as told. He arrived on schedule at 0200 hours. He saw that the enemy was directly below, sound asleep, tanks dismounted, guns not even assembled. He thought, "If we wait for ten minutes one of my men may make a sound, and before we could get down the ridge, the enemy could be alerted to full strength." So he, thinking that the general had made an error, sent all his men down the hill to engage in the acts of death. When they reached the bottom at precisely 0202 hours, the air was filled with artillery shells from the allied guns many miles away—an all-out attack. Everyone died but the platoon leader. At 0210 hours the shelling stopped. At 0211, amid the stony silence, the platoon leader said but one thing: "I didn't know what the general knew."

If we are not careful, one day we all could realize, with unbearable agony, that we didn't know what the general knew. As soon as we stop seeking his advice, we may be standing under the artillery fire.

Next time you get yourself into a situation in which you're about to throw some mud or lose some ground, remind yourself that advice given is worth thinking about, and is perhaps something you could discuss with the Lord.

Let me give one last thought: "Fear not, little children, for you are mine, and I have overcome the world, and you are of them that my Father hath given unto me; And none of them that my Father hath given me shall be lost." (D&C 50:41.) In other words, none of us is ever alone; we can always leave our burdens at his feet.

None of the children that the Father gives to the Savior shall be lost. This I believe and know, and for this I am grateful.

11

Active Gratitude

If I were to ask you today to identify what you consider to be the mother of all virtues, what would you say? What is that great characteristic which seems to lay the foundation for all the rest? Humility? Obedience? Kindness? Patience? Well, Cicero identified it. As the mother of virtue, he lists gratitude! Consider his answer for a moment—gratitude. My interest in this great quality was rekindled as I was going through my files just the other day. I came upon two items which once again set me pondering the need for gratitude in our world, and the miracle it brings, both to those who give it and those who receive it. The first item I discovered is a poem, one of my favorites. It's entitled, "The World Is Mine."

> Today upon a bus I saw
> A lovely maid with golden hair;

I envied her, she seemed so sweet,
And wished I were as fair.
When suddenly she rose to leave,
I saw her hobble down the aisle;
She had one foot and wore a crutch,
But as she passed, a smile.
Oh, God, forgive me when I whine,
I have two feet, the world is mine!

And then I stopped to buy some sweets,
The lad who sold them had such charm.
I talked to him—he said to me,
"It's nice to talk with folks like you.
You see," he said, "I'm blind."
Oh, God, forgive me when I whine,
I have two eyes, the world is mine!

Then walking down the street I saw
A child with eyes of blue.
He stood and watched the others play,
It seemed he knew not what to do.
I stopped a moment, then I said,
"Why don't you join the others, dear?"
He looked ahead without a word,
And then I knew he could not hear.
Oh, God, forgive me when I whine,
I have two ears, the world is mine!

With feet to take me where I'd go,
With eyes to see the sunset's glow,
With ears to hear what I would know,
Oh, God, forgive me when I whine;
I'm blessed indeed, the world is mine.

Oh, how wonderful it is to have the gift of gratitude! What a difference it makes. Somehow that poem touches me deeply and makes me want to do better.

I found a second item in my files which stimulated my desire to discuss with you the importance of gratitude. It's a short quote, but probably one of the most significant I have read concerning gratitude. It was given a number of years ago by President David O. McKay. He said: "Gratitude is a deeper virtue than thanksgiving. Thankfulness is the beginning of gratitude. Gratitude is the completion of thankfulness. You may express thanks by words, but gratitude is a feeling of the heart and the soul. Gratitude is shown in acts."

Did you get the import of those words? "Gratitude is shown in acts." Now, that's a significant statement; it takes the word *gratitude* out of the passive realm and puts it into the active. In other words, gratitude is not just feeling something, but more; it's doing something about it. As Shakespeare said, "There's the rub." When we don't do something about our feelings of gratitude, we get into trouble—we always end up regretting our inaction. I am always moved by some words Frank Crane penned to his father many years ago. Let me share them:

"Dear Dad, I am writing this to you though you have been dead thirty years. I feel I must say some things to you . . . things I didn't know when I was a boy in your house. It's only now, after passing through the long, hard, school years, only now, when my own hair is gray, that I understand how you felt.

"I must have been a trial to you. I believed my own petty wisdom. Most of all I want to confess my worst sin against you. It was the feeling I had that you did not understand. When I look back over it now, I know that you did understand. You understood me better than I understood myself. And how patient you were! How pathetic, it now comes to me, were your efforts to get close to me! What was it that held me aloof? I don't know. But it is tragic when a wall rises between a boy and his father.

"I wish you were here now, across the table from me, just for an hour, so I could tell you how there's no wall any more. I understand you now, Dad, and how I love you and wish I could go back and be your boy again!

"Well, it won't be long, Dad, till I am over there, and I believe you'll be the first one to take me by the hand and help me. I know that among the richest, most priceless things on earth, and the thing least understood, is that mighty love and tenderness and craving to help which a father feels towards his boy, for I have a boy of my own. Up there, somewhere in the silence, hear me, Dad, and believe me."

Well, I find my feelings divided every time I read that. I find it refreshing that a good man finally found gratitude for a good father. But I find myself wishing that he had felt it earlier and had done something about it then. We all have that same choice, to start *feeling* something because of all we have, and then to *do* something about it. That action can be rewarding.

I remember reading the story of a woman who taught school for many years. After she retired, one of her students wrote her a letter of gratitude. This is her reply:

"My dear Willie, I cannot tell you how much your note meant. I am in my eighties, living alone in a small room, cooking my own meals, lonely, and like the last leaf that falls—lingering behind. You will be interested to know that I taught school for fifty years and yours was the first note of appreciation I ever received. It came on a blue, cold morning, and it cheered me as nothing else has for many years."

Imagine being a teacher, and a good one, for fifty years, and having only one student bother to say something about it. I have no doubt others felt the same way, but just one took some action. What a blessing it could have been to that teacher if others had done the same!

Looking at the positive side of that story, at least one *did* do something about his feelings. It reminds me of the Savior and the ten lepers. As you will remember, Christ healed all ten of those afflicted, but only one gave thanks. And you'll remember the Lord's reaction. After observing what had happened, he asked the penetrating question: "Were there not ten cleansed? but where are the nine?" (Luke 17:17.) I wonder if he could ask any of us the same question? It's a sobering thought.

Now, in conclusion, let me encourage us all to be grateful for what we have and to do something about it. Since I am a practical man, I suggest we start in our homes. In my opinion, putting gratitude into words is a positive action, so let's start there. How about telling your mate how much you appreciate all he or she does for you? And you teenagers, how about the same for your parents? And parents for children? Words will make a good start. And then let's move into action. A wife will appreciate a flower from her husband, but she'll also appreciate having the dishes done; a father, his garage cleaned, his car washed, his shirts done on time; the kids, time spent with them, repaired toys, the car for a night, help with homework. In so many, many ways we can show our gratitude. Despite all the faults of those around us (and maybe a few of our own), there is much to be grateful for. Let's remember the words of President McKay: "Gratitude is shown in acts."

I also want to express gratitude for what I have received: a beautiful wife, great children, wonderful friends, the Church, this free land. And above all, I am grateful for my knowledge that our Heavenly Father lives, that Jesus Christ is our Savior, that he loves us, and that life can be good. How I know that that is true!

12

Kind Words

Kind words, or any kind of words, are interesting things. Did you ever notice how different words mean different things to different people? Sometimes, when you think you just said a kind word, it can turn out to be an insult.

Some people become masters of words alone, and they rise to great fame because of it. "The pen is mightier than the sword"—oh, how true it is! And yet, would you believe that in some places in our society, if, in college, a man has majored in the art of using words—in speech education—he cannot be certified to teach school because he did not major in a solid discipline? Only those who major in solids such as history or math are considered eligible for teaching credentials.

Speaking well is an art cultivated by too few. How we need great speakers! I can testify to you that one should learn early in life the importance of the ability to use words. We call one who becomes good at word usage "persuasive." I've heard it said that "Persuasiveness is pure power." I've also heard, "One day, a soul, somewhere, will depend upon your ability to persuade." How would it be to have such great skill with the tongue that it could be with all of us as it was with those described in Acts 11:21: "And the hand of the Lord was with them: and a great number believed, and turned unto the Lord."

The other day I had a two-and-a-half-year-old girl on my lap. She was going through my shirt pocket. She said: "What's in there?"

Then after a brief pause she added, "Nothing?"

Smiling down at her, I answered reassuringly, "Evidently."

So, she increased the fury of her search just a bit. I asked, "What are you looking for? I told you that there wasn't anything in there." At least that's what I thought I had told her.

She exclaimed, "But I want those evidentlys."

Now, that illustrates one of the reasons we parents can't get through to our kids sometimes. We use words that are too big.

It reminds me of a similar situation in which a high school boy couldn't express to his history teacher everything he needed to. He was taking a test. He was about to turn in a rather blank-looking paper, but he thought he ought to write something down, so he just wrote a wise old saying that went, "Fools ask many questions even wise men cannot answer." Luckily, he had a teacher with a great sense of humor. The teacher wrote back "Those who would be wise should realize when not to advertise their disguise."

Oh, how we all "advertise our disguise" when we open up our mouths at the wrong time! My father used to say something that went like this: "Better to be silent and be thought a fool than to speak and remove all doubt." Didn't all fathers used to say something like that? I think we all heard that one at some time in our teens.

But we cannot afford to take that advice too seriously. I guess what we have to do is learn when to keep quiet and when not to. By doing so we will have learned the first rule of great word usage.

I've seen many great speakers ruin their talks by overdoing them. That reminds me of a wonderful little verse:

> I love a finished speaker,
> Oh, me, I really do.
> I don't mean one that's polished,
> I just mean one that's through.

The Chinese have a lovely way of stating the same idea. Translated it says: "Into the closed mouth the fly does not get." The tongue is the problem of the whole world. And yet the pen, or the tongue, as the case may be, is mightier than the sword.

> Behind every word that ever was spoke,
> First the fire, then the smoke
> That pierced the spirit
> Then the heart,
> Then the word
> Did do its part.

The verse illustrates what I've been trying to say all along. It only takes a few well-placed words to carry true feelings and meaning, to make a great friendship out of a bad one, to make a man out of a boy, to make anything good out of anything bad. It only takes a few words.

Witness how a whole day can be made brighter by a few words such as these. "Hello, Mom, I just called to tell you we'll be down to see you this week. You've been on our minds constantly." Another: "Well, son, I had planned a fishing trip with a few buddies, but maybe I could skip it so I could stay home and go to church with your mother for once." And another: "Dear boss, I'm so thankful for my job. This Saturday I want to work without pay. I've seen a few things that never get done, and though it's my day off, just once I'd like to show my appreciation by doing a few of them on my own time." And yet another: "Dear Heavenly Father, I've been gone for a while. I've forgotten how to pray. Please help. Amen."

Words are great, aren't they? Before you let fly with the next bundle, try to find the best batch you can stir up. Then really let them fly. Think of the best group of words you can. Pick the best possible moment. Pick the most needy target. And remember this old Japanese proverb: "The conduct of a single moment can control the destiny of a thousand years."

Above all, may it be with you as in Acts 11:21: "And the hand of the Lord was with them: and a great number believed, and turned unto the Lord." May it be so.

13

He's My Brother

Like most people raised in this beloved land of America, I was reared with the teaching that all men are brothers. This teaching is recognized by most as the fundamental basis of the Judeo-Christian society in which we live. Though I heard that idea during my youth, it never really registered as a truth until later years. Ironically, it was a truth that surfaced for me in the midst of World War II, during hostilities with an implacable foe. One such experience occurred on Okinawa, where three men died while attempting to retrieve the body of a wounded comrade. What motivated their bravery and courage? It was the concern for one of their own—in a word, *brotherhood.*

The brotherhood of man is a truth that crosses nationalities, religions, and social barriers. It is the bridge that spans the cultural differences and brings us to the realization that there is more commonality than difference among mankind.

While serving as a coordinator of religious education in Southern California some years ago, I had several opportunities to represent the Church during religious emphasis weeks at various college campuses. A typical format for these programs would consist of one or several guest speakers addressing all the student body at a forum. Later in the week, representatives of a number of Christian faiths would be invited to dine with the students in their living quarters—fraternities, sororities, or independent halls. Following the dinner a question-answer session would be held. Invitations were extended to me to represent The Church of Jesus Christ of Latter-day Saints because of my assignment with religious education.

On one occasion, as I sat down in a question-answer session, the issue they seemed most concerned about was whether there really was a personal God. Several of the more articulate students had questioned the reality of God, suggesting that God was more a "crutch for man's faith" than an actual reality.

In response, I directed this question to the young men: "How many of you acknowledge the truth of the idea that all men—regardless of religious creed or color—are brothers. I don't mean in a figurative sense, but in the sense that the person sitting beside you in your classes—your fellow student—is your brother." Most concurred with the belief in this idea, and none openly registered any dissent. I then said, "Don't you think it a bit inconsistent to acknowledge a family relationship between you and others and not to acknowledge a divine parentage common to each of you? Did you ever see two brothers without a father?"

I'd be the first to acknowledge that one does not convince another about the reality of God by logic or reason. The point I make is this: Belief in the brotherhood of man is not consistent until we recognize that there is one common Father of us all. Once that truth is recognized, we can understand what the Apostle Paul meant when he said that God "hath made of one blood all nations of men . . . to dwell on all the face of the earth. . . . In him we live, . . . and have our being. . . . For as much then as we are the offspring of God, we ought not to think that the Godhead is like unto [anything else]." (Acts 17:26, 28—29.)

We are all sons and daughters of God; he is our Father and we are brothers and sisters all. Once that truth illuminates the minds of men, wars will cease, domestic quarrels will stop, and all will be able to come to grips with the answer to that perennial question, "Who am I?" Each will know for himself. Accepting ourselves for what we really are, offspring of eternal parentage, we can then begin to see our fellow beings as members of one eternal family.

I challenge you to train one generation in this lofty ideal—this fundamental of all truths—and you will have promise of a new society. Nourish a generation on this truth, and you will have produced a generation of unselfishness. And heaven knows how much unselfishness is needed in today's world.

The expression may seem trivial, even trite, but it is nevertheless true—each day a new generation is born.

Another generation is shortly behind your own, and soon you will be listening to its melodies, songs, and hymns. Will they be hymns of hate, hostility, and malice? Or will youth be singing of love, fraternity, and brotherhood? Personally, I'm confident that the day of brotherhood is dawning.

14

With Malice Toward None

I remember wondering as a small boy if I would ever grow up. Everyone and everything seemed big. Size seemed to be everything. Well, I finally grew up, as we all do, and size now seems very relative.

I also remember reading of a woman who stood four feet, ten inches high. She was small physically, but in every other way she stood taller than most. She had a handicapped son who was a challenge. But she had such patience and love for him that, if compared to her, some of us would measure rather small. I learned that size is relative.

I suppose the reason I have size on my mind is because of another article I read. Although I do not know the author, the meaning of the article is significant. It said in part: "A person's ability to forgive is in proportion to the greatness of his soul. Little men cannot forgive."

Whoever wrote that passage knew something that some people on this earth never learn. Read his last sentence again: "Little men cannot forgive."

As I sat pondering that statement, I pictured myself measured against the judgment wall. I wondered how tall I really stood. I often wonder. And how about you? How about *us*? How tall do we stand in our forgiveness of those who offend us? That is one of the great challenges we face in this life. It was Alexander Pope who said: "To err is human, to forgive is absolutely unthinkable." Now, perhaps that isn't *exactly* what he said, but that's what I read on the T-shirt of a young lady I saw the other day.

Allow me now to give Alexander Pope a little more respect. In actuality he said: "To err is human, to forgive is divine." As I have observed life these many years, to forgive certainly is divine. This statement teaches a great gospel principle, but it is difficult to put into practice.

Some in our human family really do have a difficult time forgiving and forgetting. It seems like such a simple task, but it is so hard to do. I am reminded of one young man who had problems in the realm of forgiving and forgetting.

During the Civil War, a number of Confederate prisoners were held at a western military post under fairly reasonable conditions. Most of them appeared to appreciate the situation, but one fellow wasn't reconciled to his captivity, and took every opportunity to express his views. He rubbed it in about the Battle of Chickamauga, which had had disastrous results for the Federal forces.

Finally, his harping got under the skin of the Union men, and they complained to General Grant, who had the prisoner brought before him.

"Look here," Grant said, "you are being very insulting to the men here, with your constant references to the Battle of Chickamauga. Now, you've either got to take the oath of allegiance to the United States, or you'll be sent to a Northern prison. Make up your mind."

The prisoner took some time to come to a decision. Finally he said, "I reckon, General, I'll take the oath."

The oath was duly administered. Then the subdued soldier asked if he might speak.

"Yes," said Grant, "what is it?"

"I was just thinking, General, those rebels certainly did give us a rough time at Chickamauga, didn't they?"

Ah yes, perspective is everything.

As I have contemplated the life of the Savior, I have wondered what was the most difficult for him: the rejection by his own people? His betrayal by Judas? The drops of blood at Gethsemane? The nails that pierced his hands and feet? Perhaps there was another aspect of those final days which took great courage. None of us can compare or know exactly how much fortitude it did take, but this much we know: by suffering all of these difficulties, he set an example worthy of our deepest consideration. While hanging on the cross, in indescribable misery, these words were given in complete love, "Father, forgive them; for they know not what they do" (Luke 23:34).

Though I do not fully comprehend it, I do know that here he taught one of the greatest principles in all of the gospel. I also know that to follow his example is a great test. William Jennings Bryan observed that "revenge seems to be natural with man; it is human to want to get even with an enemy."

When we are able to control that impulse we have

taken the first step in learning how to forgive and, eventually, forget. Confucius put it this way: "To be wronged or robbed is nothing unless you continue to remember it."

One of the great heroes of my life is Abraham Lincoln. He did and said so much that I would like to emulate. He was a living example of how to forgive. He was a tall man in every way. Out of the tragedy of a terrible civil war he spoke of peace, comfort, and forgiveness: "With malice toward none, with charity for all . . . let us . . . bind up the wounds."

That's what forgiveness is all about—binding up wounds. Forgiveness binds up not only the wounds of the offended, but also of the offender.

I know that there is no foolproof formula to learn how to forgive, but let me suggest a few things that may help:

1. Decide *now* that we really do want to learn to forgive and forget.

2. Commit ourselves *now* to stop looking for offenses.

3. Determine *now* that we won't react when offenses do come.

4. Start in our own families.

5. Practice, practice, practice.

That's not a very complicated system, but it will give us a start. I figure that if I take my own advice, I can be well on my way to learning this great lesson by the time I'm eighty.

Now, may I share one final bit of advice? I know that our Father in Heaven wants us to forgive. As we learn to forgive, our own forgiveness by him is assured. Little by little, day by day, we can do it. We all stand in need of forgiveness, but we also need to learn how to forgive others.

There is one more key I feel impressed to note. If we will go willingly to our Father and ask for his help, he will give it. Our patience will increase, our understanding of others will broaden, and because we will see how much we need to be forgiven, we will begin to realize how much we need to forgive.

It is my hope that we all may stand tall. May our measurement in the virtue of forgiveness be as large as our Heavenly Father would desire for us.

15

Stained
Glass Windows

In my assignment in the Church, I have been blessed with the opportunity of traveling throughout the world. I have visited with wonderful people all over this earth and it has been a rewarding experience. In the process of this travel, I have also spoken in chapels of all shapes and sizes from Sydney, Australia to Seattle, Washington; from London, England to Las Vegas, Nevada; from Rio de Janeiro to Rochester, New York. And while the spirit of the Lord is the same everywhere I go, I have enjoyed the physical differences in the church buildings themselves. Some are modern and some are old, some large and some small, some are rented or borrowed, but of all the sacred buildings I have had the privilege of visiting, I must admit to a bias. For me, there is a special beauty in the older buildings with stained glass windows. As a boy, I can remember being in chapels with sacred scenes artistically fashioned in colored glass. I recall looking at those windows while the sun from outside brought life to them. Even as a young man with baseball on my mind I could appreciate such beauty.

But even as a boy, I could see that from the outside of the church those windows were not as beautiful—they never are. People pass by those windows and see little beauty. Those who hear about the beauty of stained glass windows and then see them from the outside are often disappointed. At first glance, the windows will be judged as anything but attractive. But once inside, viewed against the light from outdoors, the plain-looking colored glass becomes a work of art.

I suppose you are way ahead of me about the point I want to make. It seems to me that every soul around us is like a stained glass window. Viewed from the exterior, we often judge people to be less than they are. Inside, each one is a child of God with infinite beauty and potential. Our challenge is well stated by John: "Judge not according to the appearance, but judge righteous judgment" (John 7:24). Indeed, that is a challenge! It is impossible not to judge. Decisions must be made. The trick is to judge righteously. I submit that once we understand that those around us are all as potentially beautiful as stained glass, we're on our way.

I recall reading about a church that was in need of a new pastor. One of the elders was interested in knowing just what kind of minister the congregation desired. He wrote a letter to the hiring committee as if he were applying for the position. You judge for yourself what kind of minister he would be.

"Gentlemen: Understanding that your pulpit is vacant, I should like to apply for the position. I have many qualifications that I think you would appreciate. I have been blessed to preach with power and have had some success as a writer. Some say that I am a good organizer. I have been a leader in most places I have gone.

"Some folks, however, have some things against me. I am over fifty years of age. I have never preached in one place for more than three years at a time. In some places I have left town, after my work caused riots and disturbances. I have to admit that I have been in jail three or four times, but not because of any real wrong doing. My health is not too good, though I still get a good deal done. I have had to work at my trade to help pay my way. The churches I have preached in have been small, though located in several large cities.

"I have not gotten along too well with the religious leaders in different towns where I have preached. In fact, some of them have threatened me, taken me to court, and even attacked my physically.

"I am not too good at keeping records. I have even been known to forget whom I have baptized. However, if you can use me, I shall do my best for you, even if I have to work to help with my support."

What do you think? Do you see any beauty shining through the stained glass? Well, the committee certainly did not. They were not interested in any "unhealthy, contentious, trouble-making, absent-minded, ex-jail-bird." For them, and for some of us, the qualifications of this man seem absurd. But to the Lord, who knew him, the Apostle Paul would be just fine for the position.

Making "righteous judgments" takes some practice. I love people and I love watching them. It's a hobby with me. And if there is one thing I've learned, it's that first appearances don't mean much. You may recall the words of the Lord when selecting as king a young boy named

David "For man looketh on the outward appearance, but the Lord looketh on the heart" (1 Samuel 16:7). David certainly was not the obvious choice, but he was the right choice.

It's too bad we can't do as Edwin T. Dahlberg once suggested. In order to have us better understand one another, he longed to have us swap places with each other for awhile. In his own words: "Every doctor should have an operation, every policeman and minister spend a number of months in jail, and every industrialist become a labor union member." We could carry that to extremes, but the idea has merit.

Since switching places is not practical, I think we can do *something* to help us look beyond the obvious, to make righteous judgment. Perhaps most importantly, we can remember the simple analogy of our stained glass windows. We all really are children of our Heavenly Father. There is beauty in every soul, there is value in every human being — without exception. Then, with that knowledge, let's hold off judging on first sight. Let's wait, watch, listen, and be patient. I bear testimony that if we do so we'll be surprised, even shocked, at what we find. Even those we seem to know best will take on new beauty: Parents, children, friends.

Let me conclude by challenging each one of us to take seriously this brief discussion on judging. The Lord knows we will be called on to make judgments, but as often as possible, let us make them only after time and effort have taken us inside the chapel and we have gazed at those windows against the light of truth.

May God bless us to understand that we are all his. Every living soul is his son or daughter. May we begin to understand that and treat each other accordingly.

16

All Are Alike

And he inviteth them all to come unto him and partake of his goodness; and he denieth none that come unto him, black and white, bond and free, male and female; and he remembereth the heathen; and all are alike unto God, both Jew and Gentile" (2 Nephi 26:33).

I read that scripture and after I had read it once, I read it again. I have read it many times, but on that particular evening it seemed to bear down on my mind. I repeat it again:

"And he inviteth them all to come unto him and partake of his goodness; and he denieth none that come unto him, black and white, bond and free, male and female; and he remembereth the heathen; and all are alike unto God, both Jew and Gentile" (2 Nephi 26:33).

If, in fact, "all are alike unto God," the implications are great for you and me and for our children. If all nationalities, colors, cultures, and peoples are literally God's children, then we have a way to go in showing it to each other. There is no doubt in my mind that we are all sons and daughters of the same heavenly parents. There is absolutely no doubt in his mind either. Now, if we can just convince the world.

Attempting to do something about this can be both exciting and discouraging, but it must begin. If our world has any hope of making it into the next century, it's time to start thinking of each other as brothers. The first attempts can even be painful, but growth often involves pain.

From my own travels, from my experiences in the armed services during wartime, and from other of life's many situations, I have found that one of the greatest foes of brotherhood is fear. The unknown is difficult to deal with. I have witnessed examples of this many times as I have watched my teenage daughters pace nervously while waiting for their dates. The unknown was terrifying to them, but usually, once the ice was broken, conversations were started, common ground was discovered, and self-consciousness was overcome, friendships proceeded and security was established.

I have a good friend who is in education. Recently, he was part of a group who entertained the Minister of Education and his colleagues from Communist China. It was a singular opportunity, but certainly not an easy task. At the concluding evening's dinner, my friend sat at a table with five or six Chinese. Let me tell you the story in his own words:

"We all sat at the table that night and fidgeted nervously as each course of the meal was served. Even our guests felt the tension. I suppose it wasn't so much that they were Chinese as it was that they were communists. Since almost all of the delegation spoke English, we involved ourselves in small talk as we ate our food. I felt awkward and hoped they couldn't tell. Almost inadvertently, I hit upon something that changed the whole tone of our conversation and opened a discussion that could otherwise never have occurred. I simply blurted out, 'Do any of you have children?' That did it! All of a sudden there were wallets and pictures and stories all over the place. Each proudly told of his family. I took my turn. And then, without even being aware, we were not Chinese or American, communist or capitalist, we were simply dads. From there, we branched into observations about education, politics, food, and even religion. And when we parted and shook hands, there was a feeling of brotherhood that I thought could never be possible."

During World War II, I was involved in the fighting that took place on the little island of Okinawa. It was literally covered with caves, in which the enemy stored ammunition, gasoline, food, and similar necessities. Frequently the Japanese surrounded us at night and took over these positions. It was like starting the battle over, so we closed some of the caves by throwing dynamite charges into them. One day, while looking for souvenirs, I walked into one of these abandoned places that we had not closed. As I got twenty-five yards into the opening, I walked into the presence of a Japanese infantryman. We stood looking at each other. He seemed equally surprised, and then he did what I thought was a gracious thing—he threw down his rifle and surrendered. I motioned for him to move toward the opening of the cave and as he did, he stumbled and fell. I noticed he had been wounded in the abdomen. As I turned him over, he threw his arms in front of his face in a gesture that showed he feared I would take his life. His wounds were very serious. I gave him a drink of water, which surprised him, and poured sulfanilamide powder into his wound and tried to give him a little physical comfort.

Another soldier passed the opening of the cave and I summoned him in. He sent for a medic, and with him came a Japanese interpreter. The wounded soldier's name was Masou Watanabe and he came from Osaka, Japan. As I interrogated him, with the help of the interpreter, I learned he had been drafted when he was twelve years old and at thirteen he had been sent to fight in China. At sixteen he was brought to Okinawa. He had a brother in the Japanese Air Corps whom he hadn't heard from for many months and he was very worried about him. He asked whether the American forces had bombed Osaka. I wasn't sure. He wanted to study law and marry his girl-friend who was waiting for him at home. To my great surprise, he loved American baseball, and we had the same favorite major league player, Lou Gehrig.

Do you know what I discovered? We both felt that had World War II been left to us we would have quickly shaken hands and hurried home. War seems to take peace, gentleness, and brotherly love, and mix them all up. I have thought since that if the world heard, understood, and practiced the gospel of Jesus Christ, we could literally have peace on earth.

I want to stress the words, *There was a feeling of brotherhood.* Despite race, language, and belief, at least for a period of time, barriers went down and acceptance went up. If it can happen with my friend and the Chinese communists, the Japanese soldier and the American soldier, it can happen anywhere and everywhere. So who starts it? You guessed it—you and I. If we don't, nobody will. Nobody else has the understanding of the true brotherhood of mankind that we do.

C. S. Lewis was a brilliant writer, and he was able to put into words a truly profound concept of how we should treat each other. He said:

"It is a serious thing to live in a society of possible gods and goddesses, to remember that the dullest and most uninteresting person you talk to may one day be a creature which . . . you would be strongly tempted to worship, or else a horror and a corruption such as you now meet, if at all, only in a nightmare. All day long we are, in some degree, helping each other to one or the other of these destinations. It is in the light of these over-whelming possibilities, it is with the awe and circumspec-tion proper to them, that we should conduct all our deal-ings with one another, all friendships, all loves, all play, all politics. There are no *ordinary* people. You have never talked to a mere mortal. Nations, cultures, arts, civilization—these are mortal, and their life is to ours as the life of a gnat. But it is immortals whom we joke with, work with, marry, snub, and exploit—immortal horrors or everlasting splendours." (C. S. Lewis, *The Weight of Glory and Other Addresses* [Grand Rapids, Michigan: William B. Eerdmans Publishing Company, 1965], pp. 14–15.)

It is to the goal of "everlasting splendors" that I had such feelings as I read that opening scripture. I have a desire to use my influence to get you to use your influ-ence so that we can use our influence in the quest for better understanding between peoples.

May I suggest a couple of very practical steps we can take to help bring this all about. The first one involves our children and grandchildren. Barriers can be broken down by children if we will let them. That's the least we can do. Even if we have our own prejudices, we can begin to encourage our young families to be tolerant. We can help them understand the eternal nature of all of God's children. That may sound like we're being hypocritical, but we have to start somewhere. In helping our children, we may begin to erase our own biases. That is not a bad way to begin.

Second, let us seriously ponder these verses from Acts:

"Of a truth I perceive that God is no respecter of persons:

"But in every nation he that feareth him, and worketh righteousness, is accepted with him." (Acts 10:34—35.) Let's think seriously about it. The Holy Ghost will bear witness to our souls that it is true. That is exactly what happened to me that night as I read. The Lord will accept us as we begin to accept his children. That acceptance, together with our own good works, will make us better than we have ever been, and it will eventually lead us back to our Heavenly Father. In the process we will bring with us our friends who are both "black and white, bond and free, male and female." For truly, "all are alike unto God."

17

Reaching Out

There are many ways to get cheated. We've all felt the pangs of hurt when that happens. On occasion, we may have been the offenders. One such incident took place recently.

The post office received a letter addressed to God. Baffled, an employee opened the letter and read a short but sad request. A young boy named Jimmy had lost his father at age six. He was now writing to God for five hundred dollars to help his mother raise him and his sister.

The postal employee was understandably moved. He got together with others in his office and was able to raise three hundred dollars. He then sent this to the family. A few days later another letter came addressed to God in the same handwriting. Jimmy was very thankful for the money, but he did want to make one additional request to God: "Next time, would you please send the money direct to me. If it goes through the post office, they take out two hundred dollars."

There is a moral to that story. There's nothing like a child to put things into perspective and bring clarity to a situation. After all, if you're going to help someone, why not do it all the way?

The ability to reach out to others is a gift. But the ability to do so wholeheartedly is even more rare. Once there was a man who knew how to reach out. His life seemed to serve as a measuring stick. Note this account of one instance from his life:

"During the waning years of the depression in a small southeastern Idaho community, I used to stop by Brother Miller's roadside stand for farm-fresh produce, as the season made it available. Food and money were still extremely scarce, and barter was used extensively.

"On one particular day, as Brother Miller was bagging some early potatoes for me, I noticed a small boy, delicate of bone and feature, ragged but clean, hungrily appraising a basket of freshly picked green peas. . . . Pondering the peas, I couldn't help overhearing the conversation between Brother Miller and the ragged boy next to me.

" 'Hello, Barry, how are you today?'

" 'H'lo, Mr. Miller. Fine, thank ya. Jus' admirin' them peas—sure look good.'

" 'They are good, Barry. How's your Ma?'

" 'Fine! Gittin' stronger alla' time.'

" 'Good. Anything I can help you with?'

" 'Nosir, jus' admirin' them peas.'

" 'Would you like to take some home?'

" 'Nosir, got nuthin' to pay for 'em with.'

" 'Well, what have you to trade me for some of those peas?'

" 'All I got's my prize aggie—best taw around here.'

" 'Is that right? Let me see it.'

" 'Here 'tis. She's a dandy.'

" 'I can see that. Hmmmmm, only thing is, this one is blue. I sort of go for red. Do you have a red one like this at home?'

" 'Not 'zackley—but almost.'

" 'Tell you what. Take this sack of peas home with you, and next trip this way let me look at that red taw.'

" 'Sure will. Thanks, Mr. Miller.'

"Mrs. Miller, who had been standing nearby, came over to help me. With a sly smile, she said:

" 'There are two other boys like him in our community—all three are in very poor circumstances. Jim just loves to bargain with them for peas, apples, tomatoes, or whatever. When they come back with their red marbles, and they always do, he decides he doesn't like red after all, and he sends them home with a bag of produce for a green marble, or orange, perhaps.'

"I left the stand, smiling to myself, impressed with this man. A short time later I moved to Utah, but never forgot the story of this man and the boys—and their bartering.

"Several years went by, each more rapid than the previous one. Just recently I had occasion to visit some old friends in that Idaho community and, while there, learned that Brother Miller had died. They were having his viewing that evening, and knowing my friends wanted to go, I agreed to accompany them.

"Upon our arrival at the mortuary we fell into line to meet the relatives of the deceased, and to offer whatever words of comfort we could. Ahead of us in the line were three young men. One was in an army uniform and the other two wore short haircuts, dark suits, and white shirts, obviously potential or returned Mormon missionaries. They approached Sister Miller, standing smiling and composed by her husband's casket. Each of the young men hugged her, kissed her on the cheek, spoke briefly with her and moved on to the casket. Her misty, light blue eyes followed them as, one by one, each young man stopped briefly, placed his own warm hand over the cold pale hand in the casket, and left the mortuary awkwardly wiping his eyes.

"As our turn came to meet Mrs. Miller, I told her who I was, and mentioned the story she had told me about the marbles. Eyes glistening, she took my hand and led me to the casket.

" 'This is an amazing coincidence,' she said. 'Those three boys that just left were the boys I told you about. They just told me how they appreciated the things Jim "traded" them. Now, at last, when Jim could not change his mind about color or size, they came to pay their debt. We've never had a great deal of wealth of this world,' she confided, 'but right now Jim would consider himself the richest man in Idaho.'

"With loving gentleness she lifted the lifeless fingers of her deceased husband. Resting underneath were three magnificent, shiny red marbles." ("Three Marbles," W. E. Peterson, *Ensign*, October 1975, p. 39.)

I appreciate that story.

One of the greatest obstacles of complete giving, in fact of giving at all, was pinpointed by George Bernard Shaw. He was uncanny in his accuracy when he said: "The greatest sin against mankind is not to hate them — but to be indifferent to them."

Shaw knew what he was talking about. The easy

thing to do is not to hate someone but simply to be indifferent. It is easy to fall into the trap. We are surrounded by good people doing nothing.

I must confess that I have been guilty of that kind of indifference. How about you? It would be wonderful if we could exchange our apathy for concern. And we can! May I offer three possibilities? First, we need to remember that we are all in the same boat. The Psalmist said: "Have mercy upon me, O Lord, for I am in trouble" (Psalm 31:9).

I'm in trouble and you're in trouble. We need each other. That recognition is the first step to change. There are moms and dads all around who are crying out, "I am in trouble." There are teenagers and kids who quietly shout for help. There are widows, orphans, and souls in prison who need our assistance. When we begin to recognize our need for each other, the foundation for something truly significant is laid.

Second, we can begin today to do something positive in the way of reaching out. The steps can, and ought to be, small: a letter, a kind word, a pat on the back, a listening ear. These are small things, but they will become great.

Finally, let's begin by reaching out to those who mean the most to us: wives, husbands, parents, children, brothers and sisters, friends. The secret is to take small steps with those we love. Then, eventually, we'll take giant steps with our fellowmen.

May He who reaches out to us now bless our efforts. May we find joy in reaching out. And in reaching out may we teach others to do the same. The chain reaction of such a beginning could change the world.

In Opposition

18

The Pain Barrier

I think most of us watched some part of the recent Olympics—I did so with much interest. I have learned great lessons from my participation in sports, especially baseball. So, as I watched the Olympics, I was fascinated with a certain quality I noticed in all the gold medal winners. Whether in track or field, swimming or gymnastics, wrestling or diving, each winner had a certain something that raised him above his opponent.

I know something about that certain quality that real winners have. It has to do with an element in competition called the pain barrier. I'm sure you know what it's like to work at something so hard that you begin to reach the limits of your endurance: your arms get heavier and heavier, your head pounds with each thud of your heart, your muscles tighten and scream for more power from their rapidly deteriorating reserves. And at last you hit it—your pain threshold.

Most athletes will back off here, claiming they gave their best. But a real winner will press on, triumphing in the agony because he knows he can win if he pushes on past that threshold. Giving your all when it hurts more than you thought anything could ever hurt, that's what makes you into a champion.

There it is in plain words: the pain barrier. Those who win in anything—life, athletics, business, or family—somehow cut through the pain barrier and push on. What a great quality!

I am also reminded of the opposite quality. Some of us want the victory without the effort, the reward without the work, the joy without some pain. A rather humorous story is told of one man who tried the easy way and failed.

This fellow got up one Saturday morning with the odd feeling that something about this day was going to be different. Something unusual was about to happen. He glanced out the window at the thermometer—33 degrees. He went downstairs—strange, the clock had stopped at three o'clock. He picked up the paper and read the date: the third of the month. Threes—that was it! He grabbed the paper and flipped it open to the racing section. Sure enough in the third race there was a horse named Trio! The fellow hurried to the bank, drew out his life savings, and bet it all on the horse to win. It ran third.

It is my observation that those who attempt the easy way end up third, fourth, or even worse, last.

Let me tell you of a woman who knew all about the pain barrier. She may not have worn a gold medal around her neck, but her reward will be worth much more than gold. She came in first in every sense of the word. Her story is a tribute to moms, all of whom know something about pain.

A wonderful little infant blessed the life of this woman on the day she became a mother. He was a darling baby, but he had one problem—he was born without ears. Tests proved later that his hearing was perfect, but the child simply had no outer ears. And in his early years, though his mother tried so hard, he never let himself be totally consoled as older children and his own peers thoughtlessly teased him and called him names.

The boy began to develop talents as he grew up, and had it not been for his missing outer ears might have been considered strikingly handsome. A doctor decided that ears could be grafted on, but finding a suitable donor would be difficult. Then one day the father told him that such a donor had been found. This donor requested only that the young man never learn who gave him his ears.

The operation was a success. The boy's talents flourished under his newfound confidence. His schooling and career seemed to consist of nothing but success after success. And never would his parents betray the donor's secret.

At last the day came when the son stood alongside his father and wept over his mother's casket. As they stood there, the father slowly stretched forth his hand and raised his dear wife's hair—she had no outer ears. She had given her ears to lessen her son's pain with no thought of how she might be inconvenienced herself.

I doubt if there is a mother or father who doesn't understand that story. The pain barrier is found in more areas of life than just sports. Parenthood is a great example.

Enduring the difficult to achieve something better is

not easy, but if we are willing, it is certainly possible. We all can do it. I submit that a little pain and inconvenience is a small price to pay for the joy and satisfaction that comes when we help ourselves by helping those around us.

When things come too easily, the temptation is to relax. After all, pain is uncomfortable, even for a short time. So why not get comfortable in life and avoid the very appearance of anything uncomfortable? A good reason was given by someone who knew something about pain, the Savior himself. Luke's words express it best:

"And he said unto them, take heed, and beware of covetousness: for a man's life consisteth not in the abundance of the things which he possesseth.

"And he spake a parable unto them, saying, the ground of a certain rich man brought forth plentifully.

"And he thought within himself, saying What shall I do, because I have no room where to bestow my fruits?

"And he said, This will I do: I will pull down my barns, and build greater; and there will I bestow all my fruits and my goods.

"And I will say to my soul, Soul, thou hast much goods laid up for many years; take thine ease, eat, drink, and be merry.

"But God said unto him, Thou fool, this night thy soul shall be required of thee: then whose shall those things be, which thou hast provided?" (Luke 12:15–20.)

Again, I firmly believe that we can't get "rich toward God" without some inconvenience. We can win many gold medals, but until we are willing to cross the pain barrier and give of ourselves, we won't earn the kind of reward we really want.

I have an acquaintance who recently dragged his daughter to the dentist to have some wisdom teeth extracted. She was slightly paranoid about the possibility of pain. Just the thought of pain caused her to dig in her heels, and she really knows how to dig in. Well, the extraction went well. She was given a pretty big shot of anesthesia, and then afterwards she took some pain pills to help her through. But my friend told me that even with all that, there was some discomfort and pain. In fact, there was plenty of it, but she survived.

Now, if I understand things as they really are, we don't need to go out looking for pain. It will come to us, and all the anesthesia we can take won't numb us enough to kill the pain. In light of that, my suggestion is simple: Let's be willing to bear a little pain when we see an opportunity to do some good. Let's do it, even if it hurts a little. It will make champions out of us.

Here are a few "pains" that are worth enduring:

1. Buy a family member something needed instead of spending extra money on luxuries for yourself.

2. Take out the trash instead of making someone else do it, especially in winter.

3. Do your homework without griping.

4. Bite your tongue instead of uttering a sarcastic remark.

5. Help someone who's tired when perhaps you are even more tired.

6. Do a good deed quietly and anonymously.

Well, the list can go on endlessly. The possibilities for pain are infinite and wonderful. Once we cross the pain barrier, we'll never again be satisfied with what we have had and done before.

I know that the Lord doesn't require the sacrifice of

our ears so much as he does our hearts, and we can do it. I know we can.

May we measure carefully where we are, and determine where and how and for whom we can break the pain barrier. It is an exciting contest. I know we can win.

19

Heavy Baggage

Being something of an educator, I have had occasion to read all kinds of educational material. Some of it is excellent, some is boring, but once in a while I receive something that is different and unusual. Such an item came to my attention recently. I believe parents and teachers will appreciate it, as it points out so well a dilemma we often face. Obstacles are to be expected, but sometimes they seem insurmountable. Such is illustrated in the life of an educational administrator. Judge for yourself his predicament:

"If he reports to school early, he has insomnia; if he leaves school late, he is a slow worker.

"If he attends sports events, he is overemphasizing athletics; if he misses an event, he has no school spirit.

"If he corrects a teacher, he's always picking on someone; if he doesn't correct teachers, he's a weak administrator.

"If he has a friendly personality, he's a show-off; if he's quiet, he is anti-social.

"If he calls a meeting, he has no regard for teacher time; if he doesn't call meetings, he doesn't believe in democratic administration.

"If he makes quick decisions and follows up, he is an autocrat; if he is slow in making a decision, he is indecisive.

"If he visits the classroom, he is being nosey; if he doesn't visit the classroom, he doesn't care what is going on.

"If he buys a new car, he must be overpaid; if he doesn't have a new car, he must be a miser.

"If he speaks up for some new program, he's on the bandwagon; if he's cautious about change, he's living in the past.

"If he suspends a student, he doesn't understand children; if he doesn't, he's a weak disciplinarian.

"If he uses the public address system, he likes to hear himself talk; if he doesn't, he fails to keep his staff informed.

"If he attends community affairs, he's a politician; if he doesn't, he has poor public relations.

"When he attends a conference for principals, he's goofing off; when he doesn't, he's unprofessional.

"If he checks with the superintendent, he hasn't a mind of his own; if he seldom checks, he's assuming too much authority.

"If he regularly has a hot lunch, he's not watching his weight; if he seldom has a hot lunch, the school lunches aren't good enough for him.

"If he phones in that there's no school on a snowy morning, why did he wait so long? If he doesn't call, he must be driving a snow plow to school.

"If he's young, he's got a lot to learn; if he's old, he just doesn't have it anymore.

"But take heart, fellows—keep giving your best, for no matter what you do there are those who will always say, 'It isn't the school that's to blame, it's the principal of the thing.' " (Author unidentified.)

Now, doesn't that ring true? Every profession could easily make up such a list, and so could every husband and wife, mother and father. Kids could do the same thing—especially teenagers. In fact, I'm not sure that some of them don't do just that.

Opposition is a part of life. It is as common as the sun rising in the morning, and it is just as helpful—or at least it can be. Also, it is here to stay. The Lord wanted us to understand that very basic fact and do something about it. His scriptures contain this important verse: "For it must needs be, that there is an opposition in all things" (2 Nephi 2:11).

Sometimes it takes a while to see the value of opposition. Let me give you an example. There was once a hardworking farmer who had three sons. Regretfully, these sons did not follow their father's example; it seems they had heard a rumor about their father burying a great deal of money on the farm. Rather than helping out with the farm work, they spent their time trying to convince their father to dig up his buried wealth and share it with them, despite his denial of such a treasure.

Finally the old farmer's days were over. As he lay on his deathbed, his sons came to him to discover the location of their father's wealth. He looked at his boys sadly, feeling that he had failed to teach them as he should have.

His final seconds arrived. "My sons," he whispered. "On this farm is buried a great wealth." Then he quietly died.

The day after the funeral, the three sons began digging up the farm. They dug long and they dug deep, but they found no treasure. They dug up the whole farm, but they found only earth.

Finally they faced a decision—plant crops or starve. They planted. When harvest time came, they brought in more crops than their father had ever done. After paying all their bills, they still had a substantial amount of money left over. Then, at last, they understood their father's last words.

And there we have it. Three sons gained the wealth available to them, but only after enough opposition, time, and hard work had brought them to the point of discovery. Opposition can do that for us if we don't stiffen our necks.

There is always a critical first step we must take when opposition first confronts us. Before we try to make the best of it, there is something that we sometimes fail to do. Consider, for example, the case of three men who were discussing what each would do if told he had only six months to live. The first said that he would have the biggest and best vacation at the beach he could possibly have. The second wanted to travel the world and see all the fascinating places he had only dreamed of seeing before. But the third showed an insight that quickly got the attention of the first two. He said merely, "If my doctor told me I had only six months left, the first thing I would do would be to get a second opinion."

How about that? It seems to me the last decision was the wisest. Just because opposition occurs doesn't mean that it is divinely imposed, that it must be inevitable, or that there aren't other solutions to the problem. Our first act, then, should be to try to get another opinion, to find a way around or to knock out the opposition, to try to get rid of every possible weight.

I have been in hundreds of airports and have seen what happens when people try to carry more than they can handle. Bags are dropped, suitcases fly open, tempers flair, and harsh words are uttered. Much of that can be avoided. You and I are sometimes the same way with our burdens: we try to carry too many when, in fact, we could get rid of some of them. Once again, I suggest that when opposition comes we should try our best to get rid of it as fast as possible. Go consult another doctor before accepting the burden as inevitable. As someone has said, "if you don't like the view, change your seat." Simply stated, knowledge and understanding can sometimes clear up a problem that was once considered insurmountable.

Now, a word about opposition that *won't* go away. I think we all have some of that in our lives. I do. My wife does. My children do. My friends do. Everyone does. When opposition will not leave us, what is our next step? I suggest that we make the best of it. Sound trite? It may be, but it is true nevertheless. In making the best of it, we could well ask ourselves the following questions:

1. What can I learn from all this?

2. How can this burden prepare me for better service?

3. What kind of lesson can I help teach those around me?

4. How can I help strengthen those who share my burden?

5. What talents do I have that will help compensate for my temporary setback?

Well, the questions could go on and on, but you get the idea.

True winners know and understand the lesson of losing. The purpose of opposition is to give human beings, who are not perfect, a chance to experience many different life situations. Some experiences are not pleasant, but all provide valuable lessons. Without opposition we would never learn and develop new skills, or become desperate enough to seek help and thereby find the faith necessary to have prayers answered, to have truth revealed. Most of all, we would never force ourselves to find better solutions to bigger problems.

When confronted with relentless opposition, the human tendency is to become bitter. But when we acquire the tools to make the best of it, we can learn to develop Christlike compassion more readily than we would given easier, more desirable circumstances. The very struggles that present the most anguish provide the most potential for growth and love. (See Moroni 7:46–48.)

One final point: we have all seen men and women bear opposition with great dignity. They seem to take any heavy load given to them and then bear up with remarkable strength. If I may, let me make reference one more time to the analogy of the baggage. Often, in those airports I described earlier, I have been grateful to hear a voice behind me say, "May I carry your bags, sir?" What a welcome relief! Well, there is another voice inviting us to do the same thing. His words are phrased differently, but the intent to help is the same: "Cast thy burden upon the Lord, and he shall sustain thee" (Psalm 55:22). There is help available, especially when the opposition doesn't seem to end and the road seems unbearable. When we turn to a loving Father in Heaven, he is anxious to lighten the load. He can, you know. I know it because he has lightened mine so many times. The burden will still be there, but it seems lighter. It really does.

Now, in conclusion, may I invite you to think seriously about what has been said:

1. Opposition is real.

2. It is a part of life.

3. It has a purpose—we can learn from it; we can become stronger and better.

4. If possible, we should try to overcome opposition as quickly as we can.

5. In the meantime, there is real power available to help us if we but ask.

May we learn to do this, that the true joy of life might be ours.

20

"All These Things Shall Be Added . . ."

Money isn't everything!

Have you ever heard that statement before? I suppose that statement has been repeated countless times. Money certainly *isn't* everything. But as a friend of mine enjoys pointing out, "Money may not be the most important thing in this world, but it sure is pushing whatever is in first place."

When Heavenly Father placed man on the earth, he instructed us that we would all be required to earn our bread by "the sweat of [our] face" (Genesis 3:19). Some receive minimum wage for that labor, while others earn thousands. And, while most of us work hard for what we earn, there are others who try to live on the labor of others. I am reminded of the college boy who wired home for more money with this clever little rhyme: "No mon', no fun, your son." But his father was equal to the challenge. His reply was even more appropriate: "How sad, too bad, your dad." Is there a father or son in this world who can't relate to that interchange?

At some time in life, you and I need to decide how important money will be to us. Will we decide it is all-important? Will it be secondary? Or will it be completely unimportant?

Personally, I see no problem at all with a desire for money. But that desire needs to be secondary to something even more important. Remember the words of the Savior: "Seek ye first the kingdom of God, and his righteousness; and all these things shall be added unto you" (Matthew 6:33).

Now, let's suppose that we really do put the Lord before everything else. Let's assume that you and I want righteousness more than riches, that our hearts are right. In that case, we have every right to seek for more than the minimum wage . . . IF . . . IF . . . IF we seek for the right reason. "And after ye have obtained a hope in Christ ye shall obtain riches, if ye seek them; and ye will seek them for the intent to do good" (Jacob 2:19). That counsel comes from the same Heavenly Father who said that if we seek the kingdom of God first, "All these things shall be added unto [us]." We are free to "go for the gold" as long as we will use it to bless those around us.

Now, back to the supposition. Let's suppose we really do qualify for some additional funds, that the Lord is pleased with our personal worthiness and the intent of our hearts. Then how do we go about seeking for that which is secondary—money?

I submit that there are at least two critical elements as we seek to improve our financial standing. First, we need to do the best we can with what we currently have. Our attitude is critical. Consider the example of the young bride who went to live with her husband at an army camp on the desert's edge. They could only afford a small cabin by an Indian village. Days were unbearably hot and there seemed to be no end to the wind and the sand. The young woman felt alone and lonely.

When her husband left for two weeks of desert camp, she wrote to her mother that she was on her way home; she just couldn't take it any more. Her mother wrote a short but quick reply that included these lines: "Two men looked out from prison bars; one saw mud, the other saw stars." She decided to look for stars.

She approached her Indian neighbors and asked them to teach her weaving and pottery work. She learned all she could about them and the desert they called home. As a result, she came to love the desert and learned to appreciate its beauties and moods.

What had changed? Not the desert, not her environment; her own attitude transformed a miserable experience into a highly rewarding one.

Attitudes make a world of difference. A young couple, struggling to get through college and raise three children at the same time, made the classic comment: "Money has never been a problem with us. How could it be? We don't have any." What a great attitude!

If we make the best of what we have, we will do all right. We may not have much of this world's goods, but what we do have we can use wisely, and we can keep a sense of humor about us.

My second suggestion is a must to those who would like the Lord to bless them financially. As I'm sure we all know, it's the doing that's difficult. We must live within our means. Budgeting need not be complicated or time-consuming. It can be as simple as we want it to be. The story is told of a father who kept his accounts payable in a shoe box, his accounts receivable on a spindle, and his cash in the cash register.

"I don't see how you can run your business this way," said his son. "How do you know what your profit is?"

"Son," replied the businessman, "when I got off the boat, I had only the pants I was wearing. Today your sister is an art teacher, your brother is a doctor, and you're an accountant. I have a car, a home, and a good business. Everything is paid for. So you add it all up, subtract the pants, and there's my profit."

Well, that's my kind of budget—simple. I believe that those of us who don't budget, fail to do so because we think it's too much bother. But once again, if financial security is a goal, there is no other way.

I have a friend who has been blessed financially. He tells me that there are at least four different elements to any good budget. First, there must be money for basic operating needs such as food and clothing; second, money for home equity; third, funds such as savings, emergency needs, and health and life insurance; and fourth, money for wise investment and a storage program for the future. Every individual will have to decide exactly how to do it, but all of us who want to get ahead financially will first have to show that we can manage what we already have. A budget is the way to start. Self-discipline will take care of the rest. But you and I can do it, if we really want to, if we try.

Remember, if you earn a dollar and spend 99¢, you're okay. But spend $1.01 and you're heading for trouble. Today, spending seems more fashionable than saving. What once was called poor money management has become "deficit spending." Whatever it's called, it inevitably leads to headaches for people, for companies, and even for governments. No new economic theory beats this old favorite: A penny saved is a penny earned. As Calvin Coolidge once said, "There is no independence quite so important as living within your means." Don't let your checkbook be the saddest book you ever read.

In discussing finances, there is one other question that we must ask ourselves. That is, are we willing to pay the price for financial security? As was illustrated in the last chapter, through the story of the farmer and his three sons, the three boys soon realized that any reward coming their way would have to be earned. There is no replacement in life for hard work and sacrifice for those goals we have set as priorities. Determination, tenacity, and a focus of purpose, coupled with a willingness to work hard and give all, may be what is required. Remember, though, that as we go about the business of life, the price we pay should never be so high that it compromises our eternal perspective.

Let me summarize what I believe about being financially independent: It's great! But in order to become so, we need to understand that the Lord blesses those who help themselves. Let us help ourselves by keeping a proper attitude toward money and by carefully budgeting our current resources. Then, the Lord can bless us if we seek it.

Keep in mind this bit of wisdom, reported in an old English newspaper:

An editor asked his readers this question: "Who are the happiest people on earth?" These were the four prize-winning answers: A craftsman or an artist whistling over a job well done; a little child building sand castles; a mother, after a busy day, bathing her baby; a doctor who has finished a difficult and dangerous operation, and saved a human life. You will notice there were no millionaires mentioned, no kings, no tycoons. So, in our effort to seek what is second, let's be sure we seek what is first.

To some, making money is a gift. To others, it may come with much effort. I do know that a wise Heavenly Father will reward his children when we seek him first. Therefore, let us truly seek him, and then use wisdom and good judgment as we earn our temporal rewards.

21

Paths and Trails

I enjoy reading, and although poetry is not my forte, I enjoy a good verse when I find one. The following is one with a message that is vital. It has to do with example.

> One day, through the primeval wood,
> A calf walked home, as good calves should;
> But made a trail all bent askew,
> A crooked path, as all calves do.
>
> The trail was taken up next day
> By a lone dog that passed that way;
> And then, a wise bellwether sheep
> Pursued the trail o'er vale and steep,
> And drew the flock behind him, too,
> As good bellwethers always do.
> And from that day, o'er hill and glade,
> Through those old woods a path was made.

And many men wound in and out,
And dogged, and turned, and bent about,
And uttered words of righteous wrath
Because 'twas such a crooked path.

The forest path became a lane
That bent, and turned, and turned again;
This crooked lane became a road,
Where many a poor horse, with his load,
Toiled on beneath the burning sun,
And traveled some three miles in one.

The years passed on in swiftness fleet,
The road became a village street;
And this, before men were aware,
A city's crowded thoroughfare.

Each day, a hundred thousand rout
Followed this zigzag calf about.
And o'er his crooked journey went
The traffic of a continent.
A hundred thousand men were led
By one calf, near three centuries dead.
They lost one hundred years a day;
For thus such reverence is lent
To well-established precedent.

For men are prone to go it blind
Along the calf-path of the mind,
And work away, from sun to sun,
To do what other men have done.
They follow in the beated track,
And out and in, and forth and back,
And still their devious course pursue,
To keep the path that others do.

They keep the path a sacred groove,
Along which all their lives they move;
But wise old wood-gods often laugh,
Who saw that first primeval calf.
("The Calf Path," Sam Walter Foss)

We are all making trails for others to follow. We can make them crooked or straight, but they will be one or the other.

I want to share with you the story of another direct thoroughfare cut out by a politician. Fiorello La Guardia, former mayor of New York City, would occasionally fill in for various people under his jurisdiction in order to keep in touch with what their work entailed. Once he filled in for the judge in a night court. A man was brought in for judgment, having been charged with stealing a loaf of bread. The accused man defended his theft, saying it was for his starving family.

La Guardia, after hearing the case, fined the man ten dollars. But then he gave ten dollars of his own money to the man and remitted the fine. This was not all. He next "fined" everyone in the courtroom fifty cents each for living in a city where a man had to steal to feed his family. The money was collected from the willing contributors and handed over to the man; he left the courtroom with $47.50.

A total of $47.50 isn't a great deal of money, but it built into eternity a trail that is worth more than money. That example made an impression on every man and woman who saw it. I like the mayor's style. He might not have been perfect in all areas of his administration, but it seems to me his head was on pretty straight. Fifty cents each is not a bad price to pay to participate in the building of a trail. It's a bargain.

Trails, paths, and freeways are all meant to take us somewhere. So are great examples. Just one reminder from the Lord will do: "Narrow is the way, which leadeth unto life" (Matthew 7:14).

Crooked paths are going to be a problem if we get on them. Trails that wander will only delay us. Freeways that twist might take us faster, but our destination may not please us. And so it is with examples. Those we choose to follow will be crucial: they may well determine our final destination. And, for some reason, we sometimes choose detours that waste precious time and energy. I have seen great young men and women follow some questionable examples. But, fortunately, many of them get back on the "straight and narrow." Unfortunately, some do not.

Let me challenge you to do two things. They are not difficult to do, but may well mean the difference between happiness and unhappiness.

First, we must be careful about the examples we choose to follow. The old saying, "Shoot first and ask questions later," ought to be reversed. Before we take off on a path, we should ask questions. Is the example what it seems to be? Where will it lead us? What may be the consequences? In this world, caution may very well be the better part of valor.

Second, let's be cautious of the examples we set. Whether we like it or not, I think it is fairly certain that our examples are going to have an eternal effect. That is an exciting possibility as well as a sobering fact. I have pointed out on various occasions that I know I'm not perfect. My young daughters were very observant of that fact. Hence, all of my examples were not and will not be perfect. Neither will yours. But I have a great feeling that our paths can be good enough to be followed without fear of their final destination. All parents know that, as do their children.

May we be wise enough to see that the power of example, both given and taken, will prepare paths for thousands to follow. I know that if we make them as straight as possible, we will have done all that is required. May we seriously consider that possibility.

22

Getting Pruned

This past fall I realized that if I was going to do any pruning of my trees, I had to get busy. So I did. I'm not the world's best fruit tree farmer, but over the years I have learned some great lessons. I have suffered as I have learned. So have my trees. I've conducted several funerals for trees that have paid the ultimate price for my education.

I have one tree in particular that I love. So when I did the pruning, I was hesitant to cut it back. I finally called a good neighbor to come and do the tree for me. If it died, I wanted someone to blame. My friend is an excellent farmer, however, and knows what he's doing. Even so, I turned my head while he went to work. When I looked again, I was appalled. He had cut the tree back much further than I would have dared. It looked naked and forlorn. But now, even a few days later, the tree is beginning to perk up—new growth has already started.

As I contemplated my pruning experience, I remembered a story I had heard a special friend tell many times:

"In the early dawn, a young gardener was pruning his trees and shrubs. He had one choice currant bush which had gone too much to wood. He feared therefore that it would produce little, if any, fruit.

"Accordingly, he trimmed and pruned the bush and cut it back. In fact, when he had finished, there was little left but stumps and roots.

"Tenderly he considered what was left. It looked so sad and deeply hurt. On every stump there seemed to be a tear where the pruning knife had cut away the growth of early spring. The poor bush seemed to speak to him, and he thought he heard it say:

" 'Oh, how could you be so cruel to me; you who claim to be my friend, who planted me and cared for me when I was young, and nurtured and encouraged me to grow? Could you not see that I was rapidly responding to your care? I was nearly half as large as the trees across the fence, and might soon have become like one of them. But now you've cut my branches back; the green, attractive leaves are gone, and I am in disgrace among my fellows.'

"The young gardener looked at the weeping bush and heard its plea with sympathetic understanding. His voice was full of kindness as he said, 'Do not cry; what I have done to you was necessary that you might be a prize currant bush in my garden. You were not intended to give shade or shelter by your branches. My purpose when I planted you was that you should bear fruit. When I want currants, a tree, regardless of its size, cannot supply the need.

" 'No, my little currant bush, if I had allowed you to continue to grow as you had started, all your strength would have gone to wood; your roots would not have gained a firm hold, and the purpose for which I brought you into my garden would have been defeated. Your place would have been taken by another, for you would have been barren. You must not weep; all this will be for your good; and some day, when you see more clearly, when you are richly laden with luscious fruit, you will thank me and say, "Surely, he was a wise and loving gardener. He knew the purpose of my being, and I thank him now for what I then thought was cruelty." '

"Some years later, this young gardener was in a foreign land, and he himself was growing. He was proud of his position and ambitious for the future.

"One day an unexpected vacancy entitled him to promotion. The goal to which he had aspired was now almost within his grasp, and he was proud of the rapid growth which he was making.

"But for some reason unknown to him, another was appointed in his stead, and he was asked to take another post relatively unimportant and which, under the circumstances, caused his friends to feel that he had failed.

"The young man staggered to his tent and knelt beside his cot and wept. He knew now that he could never hope to have what he had thought so desirable. He cried to God and said, 'Oh, how could you be so cruel to me? You who claim to be my friend—you who brought me here and nurtured and encouraged me to grow. Could you not see that I was almost equal to the other men whom I have so long admired? But now I have been cut down. I am in disgrace among my fellows. Oh, how could you do this to me?'

"He was humiliated and chagrined and a drop of bitterness was in his heart, when he seemed to hear an echo from the past. Where had he heard those words before? They seemed familiar. Memory whispered:

" 'I'm the gardener here.'

"He caught his breath. Ah, that was it—the currant bush! But why should that long-forgotten incident come to him in the midst of his hour of tragedy? And memory answered with words which he himself had spoken;

" 'Do not cry . . . what I have done to you was necessary . . . you were not intended for what you sought to be, . . . if I had allowed you to continue . . . you would have failed in the purpose for which I planted you and my plans for you would have been defeated. You must not weep; some day when you are richly laden with experience you will say, "He was a wise gardener. He knew the purpose of my earth life. . . . I thank him now for what I thought was cruel." ' " (Hugh B. Brown, *Eternal Quest* [Salt Lake City: Bookcraft, 1956], pp. 243–45.)

Have any of you been pruned lately? Has anyone felt the kind hand of the gardener? And, did any of us resist? Complain? Sulk? Scream injustice? Being pruned, even by a loving father, is not easy. But it's absolutely necessary. The tragedy occurs if we refuse to grow from it. After the kidnapping and murder of her baby, Anne Morrow Lindbergh made a classic statement worth repeating: "I do not believe that sheer suffering teaches. If suffering alone taught, all the world would be wise, since everyone suffers. To suffering must be added mourning,

understanding, patience, love, openness, and the willingness to remain vulnerable." (*Time*, 5 February 1973.)

The Lord himself understood this principle while in
mortality. Paul spoke of Christ's development in these
words: "Though he were a Son, yet learned he obedience
by the things which he suffered" (Hebrews 5:8). It's not
surprising the Lord understands us; after all, he went
through it all himself.

Fighting against him will always be futile. I've tried it
and so have many of you. It just doesn't work. To be
successful, you must do things the Lord's way. That reminds me of a story about an old fox hunter. He had
been extremely successful, but he finally decided to retire
and go south for the winters.

Before he left for his first winter in a warmer climate,
an energetic young man came to him and asked how to
become as successful as the old hunter. He offered to buy
the old man's shop, his hunting rights, and even his
secrets for successfully hunting foxes. The old hunter
agreed; he sold the young man all his goods and carefully
told him all the secrets to his great hunting success.

When the old man returned in the spring, he sought
out the young man and asked how his first season as a
fox hunter had been. Discouraged, the young man ad-
mitted that he had not caught a single fox. The old man
pressed further: had he followed the instructions given
him? "Well, no," answered the young man. "I found a
better way."

I suppose that some will always try to find a better
way than the one prescribed. But acceptance of counsel
and the proven way, and willingness to endure "pruning"
will always prove less painful in the long run. I know
that from personal experience.

Now, in conclusion, let's remember the purpose of our being pruned. It will help us endure . . . if not cheerfully, at least quietly. Paul, who is an excellent example of one who learned how to be pruned, gave us this great truth: "For whom the Lord loveth he chasteneth" (Hebrews 12:6).

There it is. It's simple, but true. Our Heavenly Father refines us because he loves us. He longs for our return to his presence, but we can only go if we are ready, and that takes some pruning. I am willing to try. I invite all to do so. There is nothing we cannot endure with his help. May we seek his help diligently and remember that he will do everything he can to get us back. I have felt that sweet reassurance in my life. It is available to all.

23

Looking for Trouble

Have you ever seen someone looking for trouble? I think we've all had that experience. It's becoming more and more common in our day. But have you ever seen someone looking for *imaginary* trouble? Now, that's really exasperating! It's bad enough to look for trouble, but looking for something that's not really there takes talent. I will admit that I have demonstrated such talent on occasion.

There is a story told that pinpoints the problem. An old sea captain was quizzing a young naval student. "What steps would you take if a sudden storm came up on the starboard side?"

"I'd throw out an anchor, sir."

"What would you do if another storm sprang up aft?"

"I'd throw out another anchor, sir."

"But what if a third storm sprang up forward?"

"I'd throw out another anchor, sir."

"Just a minute, son," said the captain. "Where in the world are you getting all those anchors?"

"From the same place you're getting all your storms."

That story tells it all. For every imaginary storm that is tossed at us, we somehow can find an imaginary anchor. Sometimes, we throw ourselves overboard in the process.

"A New York executive boarded the subway one morning for the trip downtown to his office. No seats were available, so he held onto one of the poles near the center doors.

"When the train made an express stop at 42nd Street, a small, well-dressed man entered the car, bumped into the executive, then turned and headed back toward the doors.

"Instinctively the businessman felt for his wallet, which he kept in his inside coat pocket. It was gone! He leaped after the small man and, just as the doors were closing, reached out and grabbed the other by his coat collar.

"The doors slid together, their rubber edges closing on the man's arm, but he held on. The train started to move and suddenly the jacket tore free. The executive was left holding the man's ripped coat.

"During the rest of the trip downtown the executive grew more angry and more despondent. What kind of city was it where a man could not go to work in the morning without having his pocket picked?

"He reached his office ready to quit his business, sell his home, and move to the country. As he was preparing to call the police, his phone rang. It was his wife calling to tell him that he had left his wallet at home." (*Bits and Pieces*, July 1982.)

I imagine that there are plenty of us who have stood, at least figuratively, with torn coats in our hands and wondered where we could hide them when we have discovered we have ripped in vain.

I find it intriguing that the Lord understands our talent for jumping to conclusions. His concern for us is real because he understands that, uncontrolled, our thoughts can do us in. We may end up with more than anchors and coats to worry about. With that in mind, the Lord gave us solid advice to think about when he said: "For as he thinketh in his heart, so is he" (Proverbs 23:7).

Learning to deal calmly with situations is one of life's great challenges. To think clearly is a wonderful attribute; to think clearly under pressure is almost a miracle. Take, for instance, the well-known but wonderful story "Wanta Borrow a Jack?"* His description of the problem we face is a classic. It is worth repeating here:

"Wanta Borrow a Jack?"
by J. P. McEvoy

"One day I went to a lawyer friend for advice.

" 'I'm in real trouble,' I said, 'My neighbors across the road are going on vacation for a month, and instead of boarding their two dogs they are going to keep them locked up, and a woman is coming to feed them—if she doesn't forget—and meanwhile they'll be lonely and bark all day and howl all night, and I won't be able to sleep and I'll either have to call the SPCA to haul them away or I'll go berserk and go over there and shoot them,

*Reprinted with permission from the November 1954 Reader's Digest. Copyright © 1954 by The Reader's Digest Assn., Inc.

and then when my neighbors return they'll go berserk and come over and shoot me. . . .'

"My lawyer patted back a delicate yawn. 'Let me tell you a story,' he said. 'And don't stop me if you've heard it—because it will do you good to hear it again.

" 'A fellow was speeding down a country road late at night and *bang!* went a tire. He got out and looked and—drat it!—he had no jack. Then he said to himself, "Well, I'll just walk to the nearest farmhouse and borrow a jack." He saw a light in the distance and said, "Well, I'm in luck; the farmer's up. I'll just knock on the door and say 'I'm in trouble, would you please lend me a jack?' And he'll say, 'Why sure, neighbor, help yourself—but bring it back.'

" 'He walked on a little farther and the light went out so he said to himself, "Now he's gone to bed and he'll be annoyed because I'm bothering him—so he'll probably want some money for his jack. And I'll say, 'All right, it isn't very neighborly—but I'll give you a quarter.' And he'll say, 'Do you think you can get me out of bed in the middle of the night and then offer me a quarter? Give me a dollar or get yourself a jack somewhere else.' "

" 'By this time the fellow had worked himself into a lather. He turned into the gate and muttered, "A dollar! All right, I'll give you a dollar. But not a cent more! A poor devil has an accident and all he needs is a jack. You probably won't let me have one no matter what I give you. That's the kind of guy you are."

" 'Which brought him up to the door and he knocked —loudly, angrily. The farmer stuck his head out of the window above the door and hollered down, "Who's there? What do you want?" The fellow stopped pounding on the door and yelled up, "You and your darn jack! You know what you can do with it!" '

"When I stopped laughing, I started thinking. . . .

"I thought: 'How true! Most of us go through life bumping into obstacles we could easily bypass; spoiling for a fight and lashing out in blind rages at fancied wrongs and imaginary foes. And we don't even realize what we are doing until someone startles us one day with a vivid word, like a lightning flash on a dark night.'

"Well, the other night I was driving home from the city. I was late for dinner and I hadn't phoned my wife. As I crawled along in a line of cars I became more and more frustrated and angry. I'll tell her I was caught in the heavy weekend traffic and she'll say, 'Why didn't you phone me before you left town?' Then I'll say, 'What difference does it make anyway—I'm here!' And she'll say, 'Yes, and I'm here, too, and I've been here all day waiting to hear from you!' And I'll say, 'I suppose I haven't anything else to do but call you up every hour on the hour and make like a lovebird!' And she'll say, 'You mean like a wolf, but you wouldn't be calling me!' By this time I am turning into the drive and I am plenty steamed up.

"As I jumped out and slammed the car door, my wife flung open the window upstairs.

" 'All right!' I shouted up to her. 'Say it!'

" 'I will,' she cooed softly. *'Wanta borrow a jack?'* "
("Wanta Borrow a Jack?" *Reader's Digest*, September 1963, pp. 108—9.)

Isn't that great? If that didn't hit so close to home, it wouldn't be nearly as funny.

There is one final, critical question that needs to be

answered before we conclude this discussion. It's a hard one but one worth pursuing. It goes something like this: "So, what do we do about anchors, coats, and jacks? How do we do better at taking trouble as it comes without looking for it?"

The answer comes from the Lord. In fact, I don't know of one permanent solution that doesn't. There is at least one alternative to the course of least resistance which we sometimes follow. It comes from the scriptures. In fact, as I searched them the other evening while contemplating this subject, one verse stood out. It may seem oversimplified, but the advice really works for anyone who cares to use it. To us all the Lord gave these plain words, "Cast away your idle thoughts" (D&C 88:69).

I repeat them: "Cast away your idle thoughts." The solution is just that simple. Instead of allowing our emotions to control our minds, we should do just the opposite. We control our minds and then we control our feelings. I have found no other lasting way to success. Learning to cast away idle thoughts brings power and confidence.

I believe that whatever we think, we will become. May we learn to cast away our idle thoughts. May we control our minds. May we face our troubles calmly. And in addition, may we avoid looking for more trouble than we already have.

The Lord loves us and delights in seeing us get the upper hand on our own lives. May we do so through constant, diligent practice.

24

Show Him Your Hands

A friend of mine, Jeffrey R. Holland, once told of a situation that I think is appropriate to share.

He said he had heard the story of a man in an eastern city who was approached by a little boy and asked to come to the boy's home, where his sister was seriously ill. Although he didn't know the boy, the older man responded immediately. He found the home to be a wretched one-room basement in a tenement. The mother had died, the father had disappeared, and the fifteen-year-old sister had carried on for the younger children. For almost a year she had been both breadwinner and mother, and now she lay in the terminal stages of a fatal disease.

They talked that night of the future, of Heavenly Father's plan for his children, and of the joy that homecoming would bring. The girl found warmth and peace in this man's words, but one persistent question kept coming to her childlike mind:

"But how?" she asked. "How will he know that I belong to him?"

As he prayed silently for help, the man received even as he gave. Looking down at the frail little creature, he saw on the ragged blanket the shriveled and workworn fingers that had kept the dishes washed and the clothes ironed and the food cooked—fingers that by service and sacrifice had brought life to a little family.

"Show him your hands," he said quietly. "He'll know you belong to him."

Now, suppose that you and I were to die today and we found ourselves in front of the Lord to be judged. Suppose he asked us simply to show him our hands. What if we were to be judged by the sacrifice shown in the appearance of our hands? How would we feel? What would the Lord see? What would be our reward?

Those are sobering questions and ones that ought to be asked. Obviously, not all people make sacrifices with their hands. Others do it with their minds. Still others do it with their hearts, and there are those who sacrifice with time or talent or any number of characteristics of the human soul. Symbolically, however, the questions are pertinent to us all.

Probably most of us have seen a copy of the famous painting by Dürer entitled "The Praying Hands." Many, however, do not know the inspiration for that painting. It was inspired by an experience had by the artist and his friend. Both were aspiring young men. Both sought for fame and fortune. At a time of difficulty, when their poverty left them without even the necessities of life,

Dürer's friend went to work doing manual labor to make a living until they could both get on their feet. But months and years passed, and the hard work done by Dürer's friend scarred his hands. He eventually lost his artistic touch. Nevertheless, he carried on until Dürer became famous and was able to provide for them both.

We can only imagine how each man felt, but Dürer was aware of the debt he owed to his friend—the man who had sacrificed his own career so that Dürer might paint. On one occasion, upon seeing his friend's gnarled hands clasped in prayer, Dürer decided to paint a picture so that the world could see the unheralded sacrifice of his friend and provider. That became his inspiration, and his painting became a tribute to his friend, one that has been seen the world over. I have a feeling that when Dürer's friend is asked by the Lord to show him his hands, he will not be found wanting.

Now, before we begin to think that sacrifice means always doing something dramatic, allow me to state categorically that sacrifice does not need to be heroic. It is not necessary to have a street or a ship named after you. It is not necessary to sacrifice your talent that a friend might become a famous artist. It doesn't mean that at fifteen you must give your life to support your brothers and sisters. It does mean, I believe, what Webster's Dictionary says it means: "The giving up of some desirable thing in behalf of a higher object."

Some of the greatest sacrifices made are those small things done that sometimes go unnoticed. As I mentioned earlier, these sacrifices may take the form of time, talent, or courtesy. They can be a thousand different things done in a thousand different ways at a thousand different times. But done over and over, the cumulative effect is to make our hands worthy to show to our Maker.

We can start with seemingly little acts. Again, being a practical person, let me suggest a few things that can be sacrificed, things that can be done on a daily basis and that have a great effect on those who receive the sacrifice. How about these small sacrifices to begin with:

1. A smile when we feel like frowning
2. A kind word instead of a cut
3. Silence when we feel like cursing
4. A compliment when we may be jealous
5. Five minutes with a child when there seems to be no time available
6. A hospital visit when we don't really want to go
7. Listening to a friend when it seems inconvenient

The list could go on and on, but each time we do one of those small acts, those small sacrifices, lives are blessed. In the process, our own hands become more and more presentable. After all, the Lord himself said, "Inasmuch as ye have done it unto one of the least of these my brethren, ye have done it unto me" (Matthew 25:40).

It is my firm conviction that giving up some small part of ourselves for something of a higher value will bless both the giver and those who receive, and the results may well prove to be eternal in nature.

It has been my experience that as we consciously make those innumerable small sacrifices, we will be prepared to offer the great sacrifices if and when we are called on to do so. Let us strive to prepare our own hands, as well as the hands of those around us. Nothing brings greater joy.

In Living

25

Counting Calories

I have a great secret that is guaranteed to make you miserable. I've tried it a few times myself and found that it never fails. Here's the secret: Every time you eat a meal, especially when you're out at a nice restaurant, count the calories of every bite you take. That simple act will cause you superb mental anguish. You have a money-back guarantee on it. I know of no other activity that causes such unhappiness. Try it, you'll detest it!

Realistically, there are some of us who need to lose a couple of pounds and, quite frankly, there is no other way to do it except by taking in fewer calories than we burn up. But calorie counting can be overdone. We can make ourselves miserable. I had to smile the other day as I asked a venerable colleague of mine the secret of his many years. With a twinkle in his eyes, he said, "Well,

Paul, I sit around a lot and watch TV, and I eat lots of white bread and plenty of sugar."

Now, I know that we need to watch our weight. I know that we need to be conscious of our calories. Wisdom would dictate that we look after our physical health. However, there are some activities that you and I often engage in that do more damage than all the carbohydrates we can possibly consume. Subconsciously, we think that if we are consistent in doing these activities we can burn off some excess calories.

To illustrate exactly what I mean, passing the buck may burn 25 calories, wading through paperwork may be worth ten times that, and beating around the bush lies halfway between.

Isn't that great?

I wonder if perhaps we spend too much time engaged in activities that don't burn calories, but instead do just the opposite? They put on excess pounds, pounds of frustration, pounds of worry, pounds of needless unhappiness.

Some of us seem to relish using precious energy on many meaningless chores when we have the choice to do otherwise. I have known people who seem to delight in needless misery. If they had their choice, they would enroll in workshops that bring out their worst qualities. Let me illustrate. If it were possible, these doomsayers would take courses such as:

Psychology 932—"Creative Suffering", Sociology 800—"Overcoming Peace of Mind", Psychology 840—"Ego Gratification Through Violence", Education 663—"Holding Your Child's Attention Through Guilt and Fear." And, finally one of my favorites, and one obviously taken by thousands: Educational Psychology 707—"Whine Your Way to Alienation."

If you've ever enrolled in them, you know precisely what I'm talking about. I know a man who enrolled in all of them and had a straight "A" average.

I submit that there is an alternative to burning calories in that way. It is simple. We do just the opposite. We spend our energy on the positive, the uplifting, the helpful.

A favorite writer of many is Erma Bombeck. She has a disarming ability to put things into perspective. Not too long ago, I clipped an article from the newspaper. I don't believe she has ever been more accurate or more persuasive in her logic. What she proposes takes time and burns plenty of calories.

Someone asked her if she had her life to live over, would she change anything. She thought about it and then answered:

"If I had my life to live over again I would have waxed less and listened more.

"Instead of wishing away nine months of pregnancy and complaining about the shadow over my feet, I'd have cherished every minute of it and realized that the wonderment growing inside me was to be my only chance in life to assist God in a miracle. . . .

"I would have cried and laughed less while watching television . . . and more while watching real life." (*Deseret News,* Nov. 26, 1979, p. A-5.)

Now, that's what I call burning energy for something that really counts. People who do that may be physically overweight, but I guarantee you their spirits are slim and trim. Any spiritual obesity won't last for long when those kinds of activities are performed every day. Once again, I guarantee it!

You and I are free to determine how we will use our energy. We can burn calories in fruitless frustration or we can burn them thinking and doing good. Or, as someone wisely put it: "It may be true that there are two sides to every question, but it is also true that there are two sides to a sheet of flypaper and it makes a big difference to the fly which side he chooses" (*Bits and Pieces*, January 1984, p. 9).

That is absolutely right. Which side we choose can make a big difference to each of us as we determine how we will think, how we will act, and what we will say. Life is too short to waste it on the negative, especially when positives are all around us. Instead of griping that we want the world to stop so we can get off, we can learn to shout, "Stop the world so that I can enjoy it longer." That choice is available to us all.

May I also suggest that burning calories on the positive has a therapeutic affect. Our wise Heavenly Father put it succinctly. I take his observation from the book of Proverbs: "A merry heart doeth good like a medicine" (Proverbs 17:22).

I suggest that the medicine works two ways: it works for the one who uses it, and it works for those around him. I've yet to see any medication do better than that.

Now, in light of the Lord's advice and the opening chart on burning calories, I submit my own:

Sitting quietly and reading a good book—100 calories; Going for a walk with the kids—500 calories; Speaking calmly—300 calories; A fun weekly date—500 calories; Making molehills out of mountains—300 calories; A Family Picnic (with or without ants)—500 calories; Letting the housework go—400 calories; Putting your arms around someone who needs a hug—500 calories.

The list could go on endlessly. Try it, you'll like it!

May I close with my assurance that life is great. I'm not ready to turn it in for some time. I believe that we can all do better, and if we will only try, the Lord will magnify our efforts. We can make a great difference to those around us. Since we are going to burn calories, why not burn them up on something worthwhile? May we be wise enough to do so.

26

Rules of Thumb

I have always had one rule of thumb that has been of great help to me. It goes something like this: "Never trust rules of thumb." How's that for sage advice? It has kept me from paying too much attention to rules that sometimes get in the way of effective and happy living.

Recently, however, I ran into a list of five rules of thumb by Tom Parker that I thought were worth repeating. They represent the kind of rules I enjoy hearing about. Let me share them with you:

1. When traveling, take twice the money and half the clothes you think you will need. (What traveler won't shout a loud "amen" to that one? The trick, of course, is to get twice the money.)

2. Wait one year before throwing out a piece of clothing. If you haven't worn it in a year, you will never miss it.

My wife found that rule a little hard to swallow. With the number of children and grandchildren we have, clothes don't sit around our house even for days, let alone one full year.

3. Never play poker with anyone called Doc. Never eat at a restaurant called Mom's. (I suggest that better advice was never given.)

4. When spit freezes before it hits the ground, it's at least 40 degrees farenheit below zero. No comment!

Finally, one rule of thumb that my wife understands as absolutely true.

5. You should expect to lose one sock every time you do your laundry.

Is there anyone of you who doesn't recognize the truth in that one?

As I confessed earlier, rules of thumb are not my strong point. But I need to temper my earlier position with a somewhat modified version. There is one rule of thumb I not only accept but try hard to incorporate in my own life.

Perhaps you have had the good fortune of reading a small book which Charles M. Sheldon wrote just before his death. It contains the fascinating story of the Ward family, who agree to try to live by life's most difficult rule of thumb. For just one day, each member of the family attempts to do nothing without first asking the question, "What would Jesus do?" The results are interesting, to say the least.

First, an excerpt from the day of Mr. Ward:

"This afternoon out at the golf course, while I was putting my things back into my locker, two of the members of the club came in and took flasks out of their lockers, drank, and offered some to the rest of us. This has been going on for a long time against the rules of the club and the laws of the state, but no one has ever enforced them. It seemed to me that if Jesus saw a crime being committed, he would consider it his duty as a good citizen to prevent it. I went to the chairman of the house committee and reported the breaking of the rules, which has raised a storm.

"Several of the members came to me this evening down at the Literary Club and threatened to blackball me at the next election for directors if I did not withdraw my charges against the drinkers. More will come from this, but what would Jesus do? It has been an interesting day."

Well, as I said earlier, heeding rules of thumb can be difficult. Now for a quick look at Mrs. Ward's day:

"I really did not know what following Jesus might mean, but my story has to do with the action of our woman's board of directors in renting a part of our building to certain parties who are allowing dancing of a questionable character to go on, together with card games that are practically nothing but gambling.

"I have known of this for some time, as all the women do, but did not want to be unpopular by objecting. At the directors' meeting today, however, I expressed my opinion and objection. The club is in debt and the amusement concessions bring in big rent. I am the only member of the board to file a protest. It will mean—" Mrs. Ward paused, and there was a moment of silence.

If you have ever been in a situation like that of Mrs. Ward, it is easy to see how difficult rules of thumb can be to keep.

I don't think the story would be complete without adding the challenge of the two teenagers. That's right, teenagers. The rule of thumb requiring us to ask "What would Jesus do?" before taking action can be practiced by all ages. In the words of the teenagers themselves:

" 'We went to an entertainment this evening. A lot of girls at the high school had been to see it and they told John and me that it was grand. But I'd rather John told what happened.'

"John seemed to be unusually reluctant to relate their experiences. Finally, he spoke in a subdued tone that was unlike his usual loud and assertive manner.

" 'Well, after it began,' he said, 'I thought it was one of those foolish things that was just for, well, just entertainment. Then I remembered what you said one day, Mother, about not wanting Mary and me to go to any entertainment that we wouldn't invite you or Father to see. Well, it got pretty vulgar, and—'

"Another silence around the table. Mrs. Ward looked at the boy with a new expression, as if some very rare experience were being related—as indeed it was.

"The boy went on slowly: 'Just then Mary nudged me and whispered, "Let's get up and go out!" Honest, I thought it would be a [strange] thing to do, but then when I asked, "What would Jesus do?" it seemed all right. So we got up, treading on a lot of feet in the row where we had been sitting.'

" 'On our way out,' broke in Mary, 'I said to John, "Let's do one more thing. Let's tell the manager why we are going out." John said, "All right, and let's tell him to give us our money back because we did not pay for that kind of entertainment." You will never see a more surprised man than Mr. Rondus when we told him how we felt!'

" 'Surprised isn't the word,' interrupted John. 'He was

flabbergasted! When I told him we thought he ought to refund our money, he didn't say a word, but forked the money right over. Do you think we did what Jesus would do?' " (*In His Steps* [1896], pp. 22–24, 29–31.)

John's question, "Do you think we did what Jesus would do?" is the kind of question I often ask myself. The rule of thumb to do as Jesus would do can be one of the great experiences of life.

I submit, however, that after practicing the rule for a while, it can become second nature. A great columnist, Tom Anderson, relates a story of what happens when the rule of thumb is continually practiced.

"The *Baptist Record* reports that there was a little crippled boy who ran a small newsstand in a crowded railroad station. He must have been about twelve years old. Every day he would sell papers, candy, gum, and magazines to the thousands of commuters passing through the terminal.

"One night two men were rushing through the crowded station to catch a train. One was fifteen or twenty yards in front of the other. It was Christmas eve. Their train was scheduled to depart in a matter of minutes.

"The first man turned a corner and, in his haste to get home to a Christmas cocktail party, plowed right into the little crippled boy. He knocked him off his stool, and candy, newspapers, and gum were scattered everywhere. Without so much as stopping, he cursed the little fellow for being there and rushed on to catch the train that would take him to celebrate Christmas in the way he had chosen for himself.

"It was only a matter of seconds before the second commuter arrived on the scene. He stopped, knelt, and gently picked up the boy. After making sure the child was unhurt, the man gathered up the scattered newspapers, sweets, and magazines. Then he took his wallet and gave the boy a five-dollar bill. 'Son,' he said, 'I think this will take care of what was lost or soiled. Merry Christmas!'

"Without waiting for a reply the commuter now picked up his briefcase and started to hurry away. As he did, the little crippled boy cupped his hands together and called out, 'Mister, mister!' The man stopped as the boy asked, 'Are you Jesus Christ?'

"By the look on his face, it was obvious the commuter was embarrassed by the question. But he smiled and said, 'No, son, I am not Jesus Christ, but I am trying hard to do what he would do if he were here.' " (Reprinted with permission from *American Opinion*, Dec. 1971.)

That account needs to be duplicated all over the world.

I suggest that adopting the rule of thumb, "What would Jesus do?" may very possibly change our lives. If they are not changed, they will be at least slightly modified.

May I challenge us all to perform an experiment? Just as the Ward family gave our rule of thumb a chance for twenty-four hours, why don't you and I do the same thing? I have tried it and the results have been most gratifying. People may wonder what we're up to, but let's do it anyway. Teenagers may be taken to the doctor for delirium, but parents will be smiling all the way to the hospital. Husbands and wives may wonder if the pressure has finally taken its toll, but they'll chuckle all the way to the marriage counselor. Bosses may tremble (even if a raise isn't offered), and friends may squirm, but

I submit that the effort will bring an inner peace and happiness we have never experienced before.

Finally, I give my assurance that such a rule of thumb is liveable. The Lord said so: "For I have given you an example, that ye should do as I have done to you" (John 13:15).

That's a great challenge. May we accept it. May we see for ourselves if it really works. It is my experience that in very truth it does work. It is what our Father would have us do, and even though it may not be popular, it will be eternally worth it. Let's give it a try.

27

Using Your Head

The other morning when I arrived at work I found on my desk a humorous article from which I'd like to share several excerpts. I am sure you will agree with me that the conclusions drawn in the article are perfectly logical, even if they are somewhat peculiar.

"Ninety two point four percent of juvenile delinquents have eaten tomatoes.

"Ninety-seven point one percent of the adult criminals in penitentiaries throughout the United States have eaten tomatoes.

"Informers reliably inform that of all known American Communists, ninety-two point three percent have eaten tomatoes."

"Exhaustive experiments show that when tomatoes are withheld from an addict, invariably his craving will cause him to turn to substitutes such as oranges or steak and potatoes. If both tomatoes and all substitutes are persistently withheld, death invariably results within a short time." ("The Dread Tomato Addiction," Mark Clifton.)

Well, what do you think? Do the conclusions make sense? They do to me. Now, for the next question. Do you believe in logic? Do tomatoes really cause death? The answer for most of you will be no. Tomatoes, as described in the article, do not by themselves cause death. Even though the logic is superb, there is something that stops us from believing. What is it? What is that something? Let me venture a guess that comes from years of observation. The reason you and I do not believe that article about tomatoes is because we all possess a gift to varying degrees. It's called common sense. Ah yes, common sense. Even in the face of profound reasoning, our simple common sense tells us it just isn't true. Thank goodness for common sense.

Unfortunately, not everyone possesses the same degree of common sense. One of the most intelligent men I know doesn't have much of that quality. Despite his brilliance, he hasn't made much of life because he just doesn't use his head.

And then, of course, there are those who seem to come by common sense as naturally as falling off a log. It's like the young woman who took three years of judo lessons learning to protect herself. One night a man jumped out from the shadows to attack her. She promptly hit him over the head with her umbrella.

Now, that's what I call common sense. In an emergency, use your head. Or, in this case, use someone else's.

I am constantly amazed to see around me successful men and women who have done exceedingly well and yet do not seem overly intelligent or gifted. But they all have one thing in common. They have used their common sense to an uncommon degree, and it has paid off.

Even the Lord has talked a great deal about common sense. He sometimes calls it by another name, but it all boils down to the same thing. In the Old Testament, in Proverbs, the writer gave us this bit of counsel: "How much better is it to get wisdom than gold" (Proverbs 16:16). That is excellent advice. After all, isn't wisdom simply applied common sense? Wisdom is using your head.

It's also intriguing that common sense is not restricted to any particular group. I have a good friend who has a "handicapped" son. This young boy has suffered brain damage and is severely mantally retarded. And yet he exhibits a common sense, especially in tough situations, that is not possessed by his "normal" brothers and sisters.

Here's another example. This particular story is about a rancher whose greatest assets were his sheep. I wish all stories could have such an ending.

"The old gentleman had three sons, one of whom was supposed to be one of those fellows who was not too bright. The rancher died, and the thing now to do was to divide the estate which, as stated, was largely sheep. The two older boys connived together. They would abide by the wishes of their father before his death, and yet very decidedly they wanted the best of the bargain, and pooled their interests against their simple young brother. As the sheep were to be divided, they thought they would make three pens, putting in each pen a third of the sheep. By the way, this little fellow who was thought not to be too bright had a pet sheep that, like Mary's little lamb, its fleece was white as snow and everywhere the boy went, this lamb was sure to go. He loved it very dearly. He thought so much of it that he decorated it with a blue ribbon. . . . Now, the two older boys thought they would capitalize on the love of the boy for the animal. They proceeded accordingly. Into the center pen of these three pens they had constructed, with the dividing of the sheep, they put all the gummers, all the runts, and all the [scruffy] sheep. Of course, they watched that the number was the same in each pen, but into this pen of the culls, they put the pet lamb with the blue ribbon around his neck. Now, it doesn't take much reasoning to follow the philosophy of such a wonderful division of the father's assets. Now, they said to their weak-minded brother, 'Willie, you may take your pick.' Willie did just exactly what they thought—he made a beeline for the pen wherein bleated the pride of his heart—his pet lamb. He opened the gate, rushed in, put his arms around his pet lamb and said something like this, 'My dear little lamb, we have been friends a long while. I have called, and you have come, and because of my affection for you I have put a blue ribbon around your neck. I loved no one of the fold as I loved you, but,' he added, 'when you get mixed up with a bunch like this, this is where we must say goodbye.' " (Marvin O. Ashton, *To Whom It May Concern* [Salt Lake City: Bookcraft, 1946], pp. 197–198.)

The first time I read that story, I laughed out loud. The last time I read it I did the same thing. Once again, I submit that the ability to use your head is not inherently associated with intelligence, race, creed, or financial status. Some have it to a great degree and some don't.

May I also suggest that it is not only *better* to get wisdom (common sense) than gold, it is also the *way* to get gold. I have seen people with a modest income do exceptionally well because they have handled their money with superb common sense. Whether it's money, position, job opportunity, or whatever, common sense is a great divider between those who succeed and those who don't.

I don't want to end this brief discussion without some encouragement. What if we don't have good old common sense? Can we get it? The answer to that question is a resounding yes! The question is how. I know of at least two ways. First, we can humbly ask our Maker to help us develop it. He helped Solomon in this way and he can help us. I know of no good father who turns a deaf ear to his child. After all, we have been told: "Ask, and ye shall receive" (see D&C 88:62—63). Second, I strongly believe that common sense is a gift that needs to be practiced. In other words, we need to use some common sense about common sense. Instead of doing the first thing that comes to our minds, why don't we do the following:

1. Get the facts.
2. Consider the circumstances.
3. Weigh the alternatives.
4. Make a decision.
5. Ask for divine confirmation.

If we do these things while making important decisions, our skill will increase until, almost subconsciously, we will do it all the time. I have seen it happen.

May we take this bit of counsel and truly learn to use our heads.

28

Turn Up the Volume

If you have teenagers, you will relate to the challenge many parents face in listening to the music of the "now" generation. I don't know about you, but I have fallen asleep a few nights to the gentle rock beat from my daughter's room. And, on occasion, parents have been known to go to the door of their teenager's room and shout frantically, "Turn down the volume!"

Now, allow me to talk about a different kind of music. When I am in church I sing the hymns, though not too loudly so as not to make others suffer. Let me share with you the words of a favorite church hymn:

> Thy spirit, Lord, has stirred our souls,
> And by its inward shining glow
> We see anew our sacred goals
> And feel thy nearness here below.

No burning bush near Sinai
Could show thy presence, Lord, more nigh.

"Did not our hearts within us burn?"
We know the spirit's fire is here.
It makes our souls for service yearn;
It makes the path of duty clear.
Lord, may it prompt us, day by day,
In all we do, in all we say.
    ("Thy Spirit, Lord," *LDS Hymns*, no. 204.)

I love the message of those verses.

Now, what do a teenager's loud music and a hymn have in common with each other? Here's my perception. The last two lines of that special hymn are significant. Referring to the Spirit of the Lord it says: "Lord, may it prompt us, day by day, In all we do, in all we say."

If we now take those two great lines about listening to the Lord, and reverse the sentiment about teenager's music, we will have the thought in place. In other words: When trying to listen to the voice of the Lord, turn up the volume!

I love the voice of the Lord, but I must admit that hearing it is not always easy. No one can turn it up but me. That's a sobering thought in and of itself. The choice of listening or not listening is ours.

John P. Altgeld put the issue plainly and simply. To youth and to us all he said:

"Young man, life is before you. Two voices are calling you: one coming out from the swamps of selfishness and force, where success means death; and the other from the hilltops of justice and progress, where even failure brings glory.

"Two lights are seen in your horizon—one, the fast-fading marsh light of power; and the other the slowly-rising sun of human brotherhood. Two ways lie open for you—one, leading to an ever lower and lower plane, where are heard the cries of despair and the curses of the poor, where manhood shrivels and possession rots down the possessor; and the other, leading to the highlands of the morning, where are heard the glad shouts of humanity and where honest effort is rewarded with immortality."

Mr. Altgeld is right. There are two voices calling each one of us.

May I assure you that the voice of the Lord is available to all. A friend has indicated that "Every devoted person of any faith who is obedient and righteous and who sincerely prays may receive answers and inspiration from God" (James Faust, Conference Report, April 1980). What that amounts to is that any person who is willing to turn up the volume may hear the voice of the Lord speaking to him.

I believe that the Lord is willing to nudge us in whatever decision we make and whatever problem we encounter. He loves to see us do the right thing. Whether it's to know whom to marry, where to live, what vocation to pursue, how to deal with difficult parents, or whatever, he is vitally concerned. His voice is ready to give us counsel.

Now, before we all think we're failing because we're not hearing voices, may I reassure us all that "the still, small voice" is not always a voice. If we turn up the volume we may not hear words at all, but we will have feelings and impressions and nudgings that are just as powerful as a voice. And those feelings come from the same source. Whether he speaks or nudges, it is still from our Heavenly Father. So don't throw away your receiver simply because you don't hear voices. Often in a storm, the only things you'll hear will be signals. But if that does the job, then it's enough . . . it's worth it.

Great men and women have always had the volume turned way up. Adam, Eve, Enoch, Abraham, Sarah, Elijah, Mary, Peter, James, John, Paul, —to name only a few who have had continuous inspiration in their lives. Others have enjoyed such inspiration at times while not being privileged to have the constant companionship of the Spirit: Luther, Lincoln, Ghandi, Churchill, Schweitzer. Then, add those millions of great men and women who aren't famous at all: Jane, Christopher, Todd, Debbie, Scott, Marilyn, David. The list goes on and on. There are millions of unsung Saints who have the volume turned up and who receive help from the Lord daily. We don't hear of them, but the Lord knows and loves them because of their willingness to listen.

Have you ever noticed that love alone won't do it? Even though a kind Father in Heaven loves us, he can't get through to us unless we do our part, unless we turn up the volume.

Let me list four things we can do on a daily basis to improve our reception:

1. We can try our best to keep our Father's commandments. We don't have to be perfect, but we can try.

2. We can do our best to be receptive to his voice and to his nudgings. We can sincerely try to listen to him and pay attention to his promptings. It takes practice.

3. We can do our best to pray sincerely and honestly to him, every day, and we can be grateful. We can let him know exactly how we feel and what we need.

4. We can do our best to have faith in his ability and desire to speak to us and in our ability to hear.

I believe we can all express appreciation to the Lord for his goodness—for his voice and inspiration. May we each understand that the inspiration of the Lord can be with us all. He is our Father. "Behold, I stand at the door, and knock: if any man hear my voice, and open the door, I will come in to him, and will sup with him, and he with me" (Revelation 3:20).

That promise is sure. May we, indeed, turn up the volume.

29

Z

Albert Einstein once gave a great formula for success. He indicated that if A equals success, then the formula is $A = X + Y + Z$. X is work, Y is play, and Z is keeping your mouth shut. Now that's what I call infallible logic. With a mind as perceptive as that, it's no wonder that Einstein developed the theory of relativity.

Silence is a wonderful quality. I have a good friend who has several teenagers and swears that it has been at least fifteen years since he has experienced complete silence. Having had three teenagers of my own, I recognize the truth in my friend's comment. Our society somehow seems to think that silence is to be avoided at all costs.

Silence, or being quiet, or whatever you want to call it, can be one of the great blessings of life. I love the story told of the tourist who spent a night in a small Vermont town.

"He joined a group of men sitting on the porch of the general store. After several vain attempts to start a conversation, he finally asked, 'Is there a law against talking in this town?'

" 'Nope, no law agin it,' replied one crusty old Vermonter. 'We just like to make sure it's an improvement on silence.' "

From what I have observed, it really takes thoughtful conversation to beat no conversation at all.

Now, while we have no trouble understanding from our own experience the value of the old adage, "silence is golden," the Lord has given us excellent counsel regarding the other side of the coin and the importance of good timing. From the book of Ecclesiastes we read:

"To every thing there is a season, and a time to every purpose under the heaven:

"A time to be born, and a time to die; a time to plant, and a time to pluck up that which is planted;

"A time to kill, and a time to heal; a time to break down, and a time to build up;

"A time to weep, and a time to laugh; a time to mourn, and a time to dance;

"A time to cast away stones, and a time to gather stones together; a time to embrace, and a time to refrain from embracing;

"A time to get, and a time to lose; a time to keep, and a time to cast away;

"A time to rend, and a time to sew;"
And to his other wise counsel on time, he adds the couplet:

"A time to keep silence, and a time to speak." (Ecclesiastes 3:1—7.)

Better advice has never been given. There is a time to speak and there is a time for silence. Understanding this principle can make the difference between a happy marriage and chaos, between peace at home and contention, between harmony on the job and unemployment, between returning to our Father in Heaven and not returning. In my observations of those around me, silence, and how and when to use it, are critical.

One final story to stress the dangers of silence. I believe we can relate to this story because we all experience similar feelings when we fail to speak up.

The story is told of a woman who dreamed throughout her life of taking an ocean voyage. After many years of hard work she finally saved enough money for a week's cruise. The amount was only enough for a ticket, however. There was none left over for extras. The woman decided to go ahead with her plans despite her lack of funds. She packed enough cheese and crackers to last through the voyage and started out with the other passengers.

The cruise proved to be most enjoyable for the woman except at mealtime. Every day, while the others dined luxuriously in the banquet hall, she would remain on the deck with her cheese and crackers. Finally the trip came to an end and the passengers disembarked, thanking the captain and crew for their service. On her way off the boat the woman passed a steward who looked at her with a most puzzled expression.

"Pardon me," he said, approaching politely, "I don't believe I ever saw you join us for dinner. You weren't ill?"

Slightly embarrassed, the woman explained her financial predicament and told how she had solved the problem.

The steward's confusion turned to surprise. Almost regretfully he showed the woman her ticket. "Your meals came with the price of the cruise," he explained. "They were free!"

Can you imagine how she felt? I wonder how many times I have eaten cheese and crackers when I could have had a banquet by merely speaking up. How about you? Have you ever denied yourself blessings by being silent at the wrong time? I have a feeling we can do better. Let me suggest two or three things that we might do to improve our judgment of the wise use of silence.

Since most of us are not used to the luxury of silence, my first suggestion is that we take time each day for some "quiet time." It will probably require a change in our daily organization, but the benefits will be a pleasant surprise. Imagine, a time to sit and think, to ponder, to relax, to pray, to be refreshed. King David put things in perspective when he indicated one of the great blessings of those precious moments alone. He said it plainly in eight simple words: "Be still, and know that I am God" (Psalm 46:10).

My second suggestion is both practical and workable. This thought is inspired by the words of James. His counsel is as good today as it was almost two thousand years ago. "Wherefore, my beloved brethren, let every man be . . . slow to speak" (James 1:19).

Well, that's it. We need to practice being "slow to speak." Instead of saying the first thing we think of, why don't we practice saying nothing? In those seconds of silence we can measure the effects of what we want to say. And then, perhaps, we can change the way we say it, or change the tone in which we say it, or decide to not say it at all. Those quiet moments of decision can make a difference in our lives. Imagine what could happen if husbands and wives silently paused a second or two before responding in a tense situation. And what could happen if both parents and children took a thoughtful moment before uttering something they would later regret? The possibilities are limitless. Friends, employers, employees, and even strangers could all feel the blessing of our silence. Those quick, silent moments can well mean the difference between eternal blessing and eternal misery. And, just as importantly, they can mean the difference between happiness and unhappiness *right now.*

The third possibility is also simple. It was given by Isaiah to his people and has application to us. He said: "Look, ye blind, that ye may see" (Isaiah 42:18).

If we really want to learn the effects of silence, or the lack of it, we need only look around. Firsthand observation will teach us faster than any teacher can. When we see family members or friends in the process of talking (or perhaps giving the "silent treatment"), we can learn just by listening and watching. The sure way to avoid an argument is to pay close attention to those who argue. You can be fairly certain that there are no silent spaces during a heated debate. If we want to see the ill effects of silence on a human soul, we need only observe the face of someone who has been given stoney silence for a few days.

I guarantee that no education is better than that obtained through observation. Try it and see.

Yes, there is great value in good timing, in weighing thoughts and words. May we begin now, more than ever before to understand and use this important principle so that we can better prepare ourselves and those around us for the blessings of eternity. In the process, we may find more of the happiness we seek.

30

If . . .

Some time ago I was involved in a lecture series at a great university; I was invited to share with my audience what I would say if I were to deliver my last message. That's quite a challenge! If this were indeed my last lecture, it would probably be delivered to my family—those who know me best and know just what I feel.

I would say this to them, as I say it to you. With all the challenge and uncertainty of existence, there is one overriding and unchanging truth, an absolute truth, and that is that God lives. With our words and debates we may put him in and out of fashion (mankind's understanding of him seems just about as fluctuating as women's hemlines), but that cannot alter the unalterable fact—he lives and I am grateful for that above anything else in my life.

It is a sad history to note that we believe we have stripped ourselves of our need for God, and stripped dignity from man at the same time. We let go of our belief in God little by little. The traditional belief of our Bible-based Western culture was always that the order of nature is subject to God, who created that order in the first place, who sustains it, and who can alter it according to his own will. But according to Kent Nielsen, a professor of seventeenth century science history, the "mechanical philosophy" envisioned nature as a great and perfect machine, created by God but now running on its own. God had been removed a step from it all. The Marquis Pierre-Simon de Laplace went even further. He changed the entire way man viewed astronomy when he claimed that it was unnecessary to have a God to explain the origins of the universe and keep it running. Instead, he proposed that a chance distribution of matter in whirling clouds operated on by gravity would, given enough time, produce something like a solar system.

Charles Lyell, the founder of modern geology, proposed that the changes evident in the layers of rock evolved over millions of years, an idea that no longer required God and the Bible as part of the hypothesis. Finally, it remained only for Darwin and his successors to give an account of the origins of animals and men that left out the Lord. The result of all these ideas was a total setting aside of the impact of God in the lives and affairs of the earth and its inhabitants. While we are grateful for new knowledge, the evolution in attitudes about the Lord makes me wonder, with Morris Mandel, if progress is progress. He noted, "After several thousand years, we have advanced to the point where we bolt our doors and windows and turn on our burglar alarms—while the jungle natives sleep in open-doored huts."

And the *latest*, as we push the Lord in and out of fashion, is that astronomers wonder if they haven't found him again. Believers (scientists or not) have always said, "In the beginning God created the heaven and the earth." And there is mounting evidence, at least for this time, that the universe really did have a beginning, a beginning in a big bang. Scientists started to note that the galaxies in the universe were flying apart at speeds even exceeding one hundred million miles per hour. They conjectured that this movement was the aftermath of a big explosion that had started when all the matter in the universe was packed into a dense mass at temperatures of many trillions of degrees. Like a giant firecracker, something happened that exploded this matter into a billion pieces—the birth of the universe.

But this big bang theory was a disturbing idea to some. Why? Because science can be viewed as somewhat of a religion. Those who believe in science believe that everything that happens in the universe has a rational explanation, that it was caused by a previous event. This big bang theory takes us right back to a beginning. Scientists are left to ask, "What came before the beginning?"

So, it is evident that whether in science or philosophy, behavior or biology, the Lord comes in and out of fashion as ideas change. In a matter so important, I think it is imperative that every human being go beyond fad and fashion and the prevailing idea of the day, and discover personally whether God lives and, as our Father, gives us laws of happiness. It clearly isn't safe to follow majority opinion in the matter, for we've seen that majorities can change. (I learned in high school that the atom could not be split.) The learned of one generation may disagree violently with the learned of another. A single human being may change his theories many times within a lifetime. I chuckled once when I read that the head of the biology department at Washington and Lee

University went out turkey hunting at dawn one weekend and drew a bead on a flock of what he thought were turkeys in a tree. He brought down two prime buzzards. He didn't try to eat the birds. "The only way [to make them edible] would be to stuff them full of cucumbers to cover up the taste," said the professor, who apparently took a little ribbing at a faculty meeting the next day.

Maybe the professor's problem was that he went out at dawn when the day was not fully light. Each of us must understand that our view without revelation is always dimly lit and limited.

Rather than following mere intellectual fashions about God and his laws, let us each discover for ourselves if God lives. Let us find out if he's near us. He will tell us. He wants to reveal himself. One man asked a little boy about God and received a profound answer.

> He was just a little lad,
> And on that Sabbath Day
> Was walking home from Sunday School
> And dawdling on the way.
>
> He scuffed his foot upon the grass,
> And saw a caterpillar.
> He picked a fluffy milkweed pod,
> And blew out all the filler.
>
> A bird's nest in the tree o'er head,
> So wisely placed and high,
> Was just another wonder
> That caught his eager eye.
>
> A neighbor watched his zig-zag path,
> And hailed him from the lawn,
> And he asked him where he'd been that day
> And what was going on.

"Oh, I've been to Sunday School," he carefully
turned the sod and found a snail beneath.

"Ah, a fine way," the neighbor said,
"For a boy to spend his time,
If you can tell me where God is,
I'll give you a brand new dime."

Quick as a flash his answer came,
Nor were his accents faint—
"I'll give you a dollar mister,
If you can tell me where God ain't."

(Author unidentified.)

The Lord is aching to reveal himself to us. He wants
us to have more knowledge of the laws which govern us
and the universe than we can ever just guess at, limited as
we are. He wants to enhance our intellect and understanding.

I remember my first overwhelming revelation of the
Lord's existence and his love for me. During World War
II, while taking part in the invasion of Guam, I was
assigned to the seventh wave to go ashore on D-day. The
first six waves did not make it ashore. Many of the boats
carrying them ashore were blown out of the water by
mortar and artillery fire. Many of these men were my
personal friends and acquaintances. The experience of
seeing their death and destruction caused much thought
in my young mind.

My particular wave made it ashore, and, under
heavy fire from the enemy, I dug into my first foxhole. I
commenced to pray to Heavenly Father to know if he
were real and if he were there. It was then that I got my
first real revelation and spiritual experience: the spirit
witnessed to me that it was true.

In those moments when we need him, he reveals his love for us. I remember the prayer Eleanor Roosevelt carried in her purse: "Our Father, who has set a restlessness in our hearts and made us all seekers after that which we can never fully find, keep us at tasks too hard for us, that we may be driven to thee for strength."

I know the Lord lives and loves each of us. I feel him near to me. About such an important matter let us not act like very learned biology professors who go turkey shooting before the sky is fully light. Without revelation we may not be able to see clearly.

In my last lecture I would also convey that every soul on this earth has worth. This has been a century in which man has increasingly lost confidence in himself. He is not sure if he's good. He's no longer sure if he has the potential to save his family or to save the world. He feels small in relation to the giant forces around him. The world that is brought into his living room every night reminds him that he can do little to change its ebb and flow. He feels as insignificant as a worm.

A concerned school teacher had a young boy in her class who felt that way. She said, "Lance was problem No. 1 in my second grade class. He seemed interested only in destruction—tearing a girl's new dress, cutting leaves off the plants, or trampling somebody's notebook in the mud.

"As any conscientious teacher does, I searched for motives behind such behavior, and discovered genuine and tragic ones.

"Lance had lost both parents when he was four. Since then he had been shunted from one temporary home to another. Only his school had not changed. Because a wise welfare worker had insisted, Lance had remained in our school through kindergarten, first, and now second grade, although his address changed nine times.

"Finally, he was adopted. Lance's behavior began to improve immediately and I rejoiced with him. Now, I felt I would be able to teach this child.

"Then, his new mother came to school to arrange his transfer to another city. The next day Lance was worse than ever before. Incongruous reports reached me: the custodian caught him taking a towel from the supply room; a playground supervisor accused him of digging holes in the lawn with a ruler.

"On Lance's last day with us I felt both relief and a deep sorrow. How I wished I could have reached his tortured little heart! Then school was over and he lined up for the bus with the other children. Under one arm he held the kind of box in which all second graders carried their crayons and pencils. As he stepped onto the bus, however, he dropped the container and the contents spilled in all directions. I rushed to help him. Big tears ran down his freckled cheeks as we knelt down together and scooped up the contents—not crayons and pencils, as I had expected, but earth—earth from the school yard where Lance had been digging these last days. It appeared he was taking to his new home the one thing that represented permanence to him."

Like this young boy, every human being needs to know that he has a place, that he matters to somebody permanently and forever. The Lord has paid us the ultimate compliment by letting us matter to him in that way. We don't need to carry boxes of earth with us and look for our place. In fact, the Lord has told us that the very reason he created this earth was for us. He who created all things, he whose intellect and glory far surpasses our small imaginations, let us be the focus of his love and effort.

This overriding concern for every human being was certainly a mark of Christ's earthly life. Perhaps nowhere is this better illustrated than in the shortest verse in scripture, "Jesus wept." And why did he, the greatest of all, weep? He wept for the grief of Mary and Martha, sorrowed by the death of their brother, Lazarus, and the fact that they did not understand.

He could have said, "Dry your tears, girls. Mortality is but a minute in the scheme of things." But because they sorrowed, he sorrowed. Their most intimate cares were also his.

A writer once said that the best index to a person's character is how he treats people who can't do him any good and how he treats people who can't fight back. That should tell us something about the Lord's character. We can do little for him. We could be ignored in our rebellion and arrogance. But instead, the Lord urges us to understand, to awake and know that we are his children, and that as such, we have infinite potential. He wants us to know that we are not wanderers on this earth without a home and place. We have a home with him.

Now, that should give you confidence.

You are capable of fulfilling your best dreams. You are not meant to be frail and afraid. You are a thoroughbred. Somebody loves you.

I want the world to know, as my last message, that just because the Lord Jesus Christ lives, and just because every soul has infinite worth before him, it doesn't mean that this life will not hold some suffering. Suffering is an inevitable part of every existence. As St. Augustine said, "God had one Son on earth without sin, but never one without suffering."

If we believe that we will someday hit a plateau in life where there are no challenges or frustrations, we are facing life with false expectations. If we think that some lucky person in our life has found that golden plateau, again we are wrong. We have merely met a good actor.

Just as we expect storms and clouds to be a part of the earth's weather, so are storms and clouds a part of life. They don't necessarily come our way because we deserve them. They come because in this world each person has free agency, the opportunity to choose. That choice may mean that someone may smash his fist into your undeserving nose and break it. It may mean that somewhere somebody may make a governmental decision that plunges the nation into economic ruin. A car may hit your child, a virus may infect your body. It is entirely possible that you may miss your dream only by a thread, a single misstep.

In World War II, I remember being overwhelmed by the suffering of humanity. First of all, I didn't know what I was doing there. All I wanted to do was play ball. I had spent many long hours in high school staring out the window, dreaming of myself as a baseball player. Then I got a letter that exploded those dreams. I was being asked, oh so graciously, to go to war and kill people. I didn't want to do that.

Do you know what it is like to be sitting in a foxhole and have a Japanese mother send her children running toward you with packs of dynamite on their backs? The women pointed to our line, hit the plungers at the tops of the packs and sent their children running to their deaths, hoping they would get far enough to jump in the foxholes of American soldiers.

We had the choice of shooting the children or grabbing them and trying to wrestle the packs off their backs. I watched half a dozen of our men, many of them fathers, blown to bits while trying to save enemy children. Think of the irony of those words—enemy children.

I've seen suffering. And I knew suffering myself during those war years: watching someone who was my buddy a minute ago become just a bloody heap in the field; having to stagger on when the dengue fever was so bad I could hardly move; sleeping all night with a two-foot rat in my foxhole.

I want to assure you that I still believe that in the long haul goodness really does prevail. Suffering has its end, and those who endure it well will learn qualities of the heart and spirit that are learned in no other way. In the midst of sorrow and adversity, if you use the laws of happiness that God has given through the prophets, you will triumph, and triumph with an expanded heart. Though there are times when powers of darkness seem to be all about us, though we face discouragement and heartbreak personally and as a world, the Lord assures us that shadows always flee before his light. Goodness will prevail. It cannot fail.

From my war experience, I had some opportunities to soothe and help on both sides. I wrestled a dynamite pack from a small child and saved both our lives. I vowed that if I ever had a chance, if ever I was in a position of any kind of power, I would try to change the philosophy and problems that had caused that awful war. It is easy to be critical or discouraged by your personal lot or the lot of the world. But the solution is to never give up or retreat into cynicism. The solution is to rise to leadership and do something about it.

Yes, there is suffering in life, but goodness prevails. It is somewhat like the parts of an airplane. Taken separately, they are practically useless. A wing can do nothing. A tail flap is useless. The engine can go nowhere. But put them all together with a pilot in the cockpit and the airplane can soar through the heavens. So it is with the events of my life. Some have been tragic. Some have been happy. But when they are built together and the Lord is at the controls, they form a craft which is going someplace, and I am comforted.

Take courage then! Be unafraid! You can face what comes to you and you'll be better for it. The Lord can comfort you through any sorrow.

The last thing I would say, the last of the last words, is this. Through your life, everything is easier if you keep a sense of humor. In fact, my favorite thought is that crisis plus time equals humor.

For instance, I know of a young bride who was cooking her first turkey. She read the instructions very carefully so as to do everything just right. She wanted her guests to be properly impressed with her cooking abilities. Well, the instructions said to baste the turkey every hour. So she did. Every hour, she took out her needle and thread and basted the turkey. At the time, it was a little crisis. But now, years later, it's her favorite story to tell on herself.

Life has so much to offer. Look up and enjoy it! A young man once found a two-dollar bill on the road. From that time on he never lifted his eyes from the ground while walking. In forty years, he accumulated 29,516 buttons, 52,172 pins, seven pennies, a bent back, and a miserable disposition. He lost the smiles of his friends, the beauties of nature, and an opportunity to serve his fellowman.

Don't spend too much time looking down, then. Don't relive your shortcomings a million times. Don't dwell on your failures. Learn to laugh at yourself. Eat more ice cream and less broccoli. Go barefoot earlier in the spring. Invite company in even when you haven't vacuumed. When you've studied don't worry about the test. Stop to look at the sunset and do attend the circus when it comes to town.

The Lord has made the world an extravagantly beautiful place where there are a million shades in a butterfly's wing, a thousand kinds of wildflowers on the hillside. Laugh and enjoy it.

So, my last lecture in this life would contain four points. First, through all the apparent flux and uncertainty of this world, there are absolute truths—God lives and reveals himself and his laws to those who seek him. Second, every soul has infinite worth. Our greatest task is to wake up and recognize who we are. Third, though there is suffering, goodness will prevail. Fourth, humor has the power to enrich every day and give it balance.

On his death bed, O. Henry asked that the lights be turned up. "I don't want to go home in the dark," he said. To that I add, I thank the Lord every day for his gifts to me because I would never want to live in the dark.